10 WEEKS COUPLES THERAPY WORKBOOK

ENGAGING STRATEGIES AND EXERCISES TO ENHANCE COMMUNICATION, REKINDLE LOVE, AND DEEPEN INTIMACY IN YOUR RELATIONSHIP

G. GAGLIARDI

CONTENTS

Introduction   5

1. WEEK 1: REVISITING YOUR
   RELATIONSHIP'S ROOTS   11
   Reflecting on the Purpose of the Journey   12
   Setting the Stage   14
   The Role of Attachment   15
   Workbook Exercises   18

2. WEEK 2: ENHANCING COMMUNICATION   23
   Exploring the Importance of Effective
   Communication   24
   Practical Communication Tips   27
   The Languages of Love   30
   Workbook Exercises   31

3. WEEK 3: APPRECIATING YOUR PARTNER   35
   The Science Behind   36
   The Importance of Gratitude   38
   Ways to Be Grateful   40
   Workbook Exercises   42

4. WEEK 4: IMPROVING TRUST   45
   The Glass That Protects Relationships   46
   When the Glass Breaks   47
   Strengthening the Glass   49
   Workbook Exercises   51

5. WEEK 5: DEEPENING INTIMACY   55
   Why Intimacy Matters   56
   Understanding Types of Intimacy   58
   Ways to Improve Intimacy   60
   Workbook Exercises   62

6. WEEK 6: RESOLVING CONFLICT   67
   A Healthy Conflict Resolution   68
   Techniques for Constructive Conflict   69
   The Role of Boundaries   71
   Workbook Exercises   73

7. WEEK 7: STRENGTHENING THE
   FRIENDSHIP BOND   79
   Why It Pays to Be Friends   80
   Nurturing Friendship   83
   Workbook Exercises   87

8. WEEK 8: TACKLING FINANCES   91
   Financial Harmony   92
   Strategies for Effective Financial Communication   93
   Workbook Exercises   94

9. WEEK 9: PLANNING FOR THE FUTURE
   TOGETHER   103
   Sharing Goals   104
   Individual Growth Within the Relationship   106
   Strategies for Growing as a Couple   109
   Workbook Exercises   111

10. WEEK 10: CELEBRATING LOVE AND
    COMMITMENT   115
    Exploring Varied Expressions of Love   116
    Choosing to Commit   119
    Workbook Exercises   122

Conclusion   125
References   129

INTRODUCTION

" *And when you choose a life partner, you're choosing a lot of things, including your parenting partner and someone who will deeply influence your children, your eating companion for about 20,000 meals, your travel companion for about 100 vacations, your primary leisure time and retirement friend, your career therapist, and someone whose day you'll hear about 18,000 times.*

— TIM URBAN

As the quote above emphasizes, choosing your lifelong partner implies choosing a person who will accompany you for the rest of your life and will fill all your days, 24-7. They'll stay with you when you accomplish great results and when you feel down and need a shoulder to cry on. At the same time, they'll be present in your routine, thus keeping you company during breakfast, lunch, and dinner and facing daily stressors and struggles with you. Choosing your lifelong companion is not easy, is it?

Well, you made your choice and finally found the person with whom you want to spend the rest of your days. As romantic, idyllic, and magical as it seems, it also comes with downs and obstacles. When was the last time you got the chills while talking to your partner or doing something together? Do you remember the old sparkle that connected you both on a deep level? After years of being together, you might miss the good old days when you enjoyed every single moment with your partner, while right now, routine and responsibilities fill your conversations and days. During the first few months and years, you might have felt like you needed to put all your effort into the relationship to ensure it developed strongly and healthily. Now, you might believe you don't need to put the same energy into maintaining your relationship because you already know each other well and are aware that you will stay together for the rest of your lives.

However, maintaining a long-term relationship is complicated and full of obstacles and challenges. You might believe you know your partner like anyone else and then discover that they've changed and you haven't even noticed it. Or, you might not have realized how your interactions have adjusted to your busy lives and revolve around your duties and daily tasks. Therefore, all the romance and attention to detail have gone away and have been replaced with empty conversations about what to eat for dinner or which movie to rewatch on Saturday nights. You might look at your partner and wonder what's gone wrong in the last period and if there's a way to avoid stagnation.

Don't feel hopeless or ashamed of your situation because you're not the only one. Like many other couples in a long-term relationship, you struggle to keep the flame alive and maintain a healthy and deep connection. You might feel physically and emotionally disconnected from each other due to all the stress and responsibilities accumulated over the years. You might convince yourself that your partner doesn't understand you anymore and that they don't like doing things together as they used to, thus feeling lonely and isolated. Like many other couples, you might believe your relationship has hit a plateau, and after a wonderful period together, there's nothing else left to do to feel joyful and fulfilled again. You might also notice a change in your communication, as misunderstandings are more common than before, and conflicts arise easily. In addition, you might lack physical intimacy with your partner because you prioritize other aspects of your life and fill your mind with so many tasks to accomplish that you don't remember to give a quick kiss or a short hug to your loved one. If that's not enough, you might experience financial hardship, making conversations even more heated and daily tasks more stressful.

This is absolutely normal and something many couples experience after being together for a long time. The good news is that you have the power to avoid stagnation by putting effort into building and maintaining a strong and deep connection with your partner.

Thanks to this step-by-step guide, you'll undertake your journey to rediscover the old sparkle you thought you lost forever and reconnect with your loved one. This workbook is simple, practical, and straightforward, as it is composed of 10 chapters that correspond to the 10-week therapeutic path. You'll build upon your skills gradually together until reaching enhanced communication, deeper emotional intimacy, rekindled passion, strengthened friendship, improved conflict resolution, and aligned financial goals. After finishing this workbook, you'll be ready to start your new life together and plan your future together.

Chapter 1 (or the first week) will take a look back to the roots of your relationship to prepare the path to your future. Chapter 2 will focus on improving your communication skills, and Chapter 3 on expressing gratitude toward each other in your daily life. Next, Chapter 4 will dive deep into the significance of trust and how to cultivate it, while in Chapter 5, you'll discover the various types of intimacy in romantic relationships and how to develop all of them. Chapter 6 will emphasize the crucial role of effective conflict resolution and strategies to face arguments healthily. Chapter 7 will focus on the importance of seeing your partner not just as your life companion but also as a good friend who will always be there for you. Then, Chapter 8 will tackle the hot topic of finances and provide techniques to talk about money, and Chapter 9 will discuss ways to collaborate to envision and plan your future together. Finally, Chapter 10 will invite you to celebrate your journey and appreciate every step you take to improve your relationship by showing love and commitment. In each chapter, you'll find essential theoretical knowledge and practical activities to try together.

After completing the workbook, you'll experience a renewed connection with your partner, characterized by deep emotional intimacy, enhanced communication, and revitalized romance and affection. The improvements you'll notice in your relationship won't just be temporary fixes but lasting, positive changes that will enrich your connection with your loved one. Keep in mind that the secret to achieving concrete results resides within you: The more effort and commitment you put into your journey toward improvement, the more satisfied you'll be with your achievements. Sometimes, you'll face challenges and struggle to continue your path together—don't give up, and always appreciate your efforts.

Before getting started, I suggest you don't limit yourself to reading the following pages passively but actively engage with the content of each chapter and put the proposed activities into practice in your daily life, thus ensuring constant improvement. Start right now by making a pledge to each other as you begin this therapeutic journey together: Commit to actively participating in and benefiting from this new chapter you're about to begin together. Repeat the words below out loud to each other: "As we step into this journey, we pledge to give our relationship the effort, attention, and honesty it deserves. We commit to exploring every chapter with open hearts and minds, supporting each other's growth, and celebrating our love at every opportunity. This is our promise to each other—to navigate this journey with patience, understanding, and a desire to enrich the connection that we cherish so dearly."

WEEK 1: REVISITING YOUR RELATIONSHIP'S ROOTS

> *Perhaps the biggest mistake I made in the past was that I believed love was about finding the right person. In reality, love is about becoming the right person. Don't look for the person you want to spend your life with. Become the person you want to spend your life with.*

— NEIL STRAUSS

When you finally find your lifelong partner, you might think they have all the answers to your problems and will guide you through your journey of self-discovery. You might believe that they'll complete you by showing you the right path and helping you cross it, but that's not how life goes in reality. To maintain a healthy and long-lasting relationship with your life-long companion, you must work on yourselves first, and that's exactly what you'll do in this chapter. In the next sections, you'll reflect on the reasons why you want to undertake this journey together, discover the significance of developing an open mind and heart, and understand the basics of attachment theory and how it influences your relationship. Finally, you'll find some useful activities to take the first steps toward your journey of mutual growth.

REFLECTING ON THE PURPOSE OF THE JOURNEY

You might feel disconnected and distant from each other, but you actually have something in common that makes you closer: You decided to undertake this journey together. To make concrete changes in your relationship, you must first acknowledge your current situation and the fact that you can improve. Take a few seconds to appreciate the effort you put into reaching this point and thank your partner for being close to you. Then, it's time to dive deep into your journey of mutual growth: Reflect on the reasons why you decided to start this journey. Don't restrict yourself to answering the first "why," but keep digging until you find a deeper reason that satisfies your desire to know more. For example, you might believe that you've started this journey because, in the last weeks or months, your partner doesn't listen to you anymore or make you feel appreciated as they used to. Is this the profound reason, or is there something else behind this unmet need? The more you investigate, the more you learn about yourself and your relationship.

If you want to make your relationship stronger, you must work on its foundations, which are mutual growth and understanding. To ensure mutual growth, you must support and encourage each other to pursue your interests as individuals and collaborators in a team. If your relationship is growth-oriented, you feel excited to plan your future together while adapting to each other and complementing your progress. You both understand that a healthy relationship allows you to follow your dreams and grow as a couple at the same time. The most significant element of a growth-oriented relationship is vulnerability, which means that you and your partner feel comfortable talking about everything, even the darkest and most hidden thoughts and emotions.

The concept of mutual growth is strictly connected with the word "change," which usually scares people because we associate it with negative outcomes. In the last months or years, you might have noticed your partner change (or grow) and feel scared because you don't recognize them anymore. However, individual growth is normal, and we can't avoid it. In fact, you've probably changed, too, since the beginning of your relationship, and you might not be aware of it. To foster mutual growth, accept that everyone grows, even your lifelong companion, and embrace change because it's part of your relationship and will accompany you for your whole life.

Understanding is linked with mutual growth, as you must be able to understand your partner's point of view to accept the way they change. If you're understanding, you take their perspective and put yourself in their shoes, thus empathizing with them and seeing the world from their eyes. For example, after years of being together, you might discover that you enjoy staying in the comfort of your house and are the typical couch potato while your partner feels like exploring the world and organizing holidays abroad together. If you're not understanding, you might fear this change and think that they must have gone crazy or something weird must have happened in their brain. If you're understanding, you acknowledge that they're just adapting and becoming aware of their new needs, and the only thing you can do is support them, encourage them to follow their passions and explore the world together.

SETTING THE STAGE

To undertake the journey of mutual growth together, you must foster openness in all your conversations because the more you're honest, the more you embrace new ideas and experiences, thus accepting change more easily. If you're open, you approach things with curiosity and aren't afraid of what's new in your or others' lives. At the same time, you pursue adventures and look forward to challenging your skills to learn something new. In particular, openness refers to the way you communicate with your partner and allows you to express yourself freely without fear of being judged, criticized, or rejected. In other words, you openly show your vulnerability because you feel comfortable with them and know that they'll do their best to understand your point of view and support your ideas. Openness is a critical factor because it enhances intimacy and deepens your connection. If you're open with each other, you feel like you understand each other like anybody else can, and you feel closer to each other because you know things about your partner that nobody else knows.

If you want to enhance open communication in your relationship, acknowledge that it requires a lot of time, effort, and discomfort. In fact, talking openly about hopes, desires, and positive emotions is easy, while discussing fears, regrets, or negative thoughts is much harder. However, openness is fundamental to facing all obstacles and challenges that life throws at you, so try fostering it as much as you can. Start by sharing negative thoughts or emotions that don't make you particularly uncomfortable and work your way up to more delicate and difficult topics. Keep in mind that your lifelong companion isn't only there to encourage and support you during happy days but also during tough times, so don't be afraid to express yourself freely and talk about everything. To cultivate open communication, focus on being patient and present in your partner's life. Don't rush your judgment, but take the time to listen to them and understand their point of view on a deeper level. In addition, keep track of their emotional states by asking them simple questions about their day, work, and personal life. This way, you make them feel comfortable with talking to you and expressing their opinion freely.

THE ROLE OF ATTACHMENT

To enhance understanding and openness in your relationship, you must be curious about your partner and investigate what makes them who they are. Do you know why they react negatively to certain things you tell them? Do you know why they avoid talking about particular aspects of your relationship or feel the need to be reassured all the time about your love and appreciation for them? If you don't know the answers to these questions, you probably don't know their attachment style and how it influences their interactions with others, especially you.

Have you ever heard about attachment theory? It was developed by psychologist John Bowlby during the 1950s and 1960s to discover the connection between a mother and a child (Cherry, 2023). Until that moment, psychologists believed that the deep bond (or attachment) between mother and child depended on the fact that she provided food and shelter. However, Bowlby's experiments proved that the parent–child attachment goes much deeper than that and is linked to the parent's ability to respond to their child's needs. Depending on the parent–child interactions, children develop different styles of attachment: secure, anxious, avoidant, and disorganized.

At this point, you might wonder how attachment theory is connected to your relationship with your partner. Well, your attachment style developed during your childhood and shapes all your relationships with others, especially your partners. Depending on your attachment style, you interact differently with your loved ones and express different insecurities and fears. Knowing your significant other's attachment style can increase understanding and openness in your relationship. At the same time, becoming aware of your style allows you to understand yourself better and improve your communication.

If you have a secure attachment, you likely had a positive and healthy relationship with your primary caregiver as a child. You felt free to express your opinion and explore the world on your own while knowing that they'd always be there for you to support and comfort you in times of need. The self-confidence and self-esteem you developed during your childhood are still present in your life as an adult, as you value your thoughts and opinions and stand up for yourself while respecting others. If you need help, you're not afraid of asking for it because you know your limits and accept them. In addition, you're more likely to build healthy and long-lasting romantic relationships thanks to your empathy and openness. In fact, you enjoy sharing your thoughts and emotions with your partners and look for intimacy.

Let's consider a real-life example of a person with a secure attachment. Imagine noticing that your partner looks distant and absent and worrying about their well-being. If you have a secure attachment, you think they might have a bad day and need to vent, so you get closer to them and simply tell them that you're there for them if they need to talk. You give them space, and when they're ready, they come to you expressing their concerns, and you listen to them carefully.

The secure attachment style is the only healthy one, while the other three are considered unhealthy. If you have an anxious attachment style, your romantic relationships are characterized by fears, insecurity, and anxiety. You're afraid that your partner will suddenly leave you and crave intimacy to be as close as possible to them, thus clinging to them. Such behaviors derive from a childhood when you struggled to accept separation from your primary caregiver. When they left you alone for some reason, you probably overreacted, cried a lot, and were hard to comfort once they returned. Your primary caregiver probably met some of your needs but not all of them, so you didn't feel 100% secure in the relationship with them and manifested your insecurity through anxiety. In your romantic relationships, you struggle to express your thoughts and emotions and be authentic with your partner. At the same time, you constantly worry that they're not satisfied with the relationship and plan to break up with you.

Let's consider the previous example of your partner looking distant: If you have an anxious attachment, you immediately worry that something is wrong and bomb them with questions about how they feel and if you're enough for them, thus not understanding what they need from you at that moment. You think that they look distant because they don't love you and are thinking about someone else. The more they struggle to answer your questions as you would expect, the more you get anxious and believe that they're hiding something, thus feeling even worse than before and risking causing an unnecessary argument.

If you have an avoidant attachment style, your primary caregiver was probably unpredictable and didn't meet your needs regularly, thus forcing you to self-soothe on your own when you needed help. As you weren't used to expressing your emotions and thoughts and grew up feeling extremely independent, you now struggle to get intimate with your partners and depend on them as an adult. You look distant and avoid all conversations about your emotions and needs with the risk of causing misunderstandings and conflicts in your relationships. In addition, you value your independence highly, so you tend to prioritize your interests and goals over your partner's or the couple's. If you have an avoidant style and notice your partner being distant, you simply don't react because you don't possess the skills to support and comfort them. Even if they try to vent, you minimize their emotions and tell them that they should be happy that things didn't go worse than they expected.

Finally, the disorganized style is characterized by a mix of behaviors that make the person who possesses it highly unstable and unpredictable. Luckily, it's the least common attachment style because it stems from childhood trauma or abuse. If you have a disorganized style, your primary caregiver was probably absent and dealing with trauma or poor mental health on their own, so they struggled to take care of you regularly and give you love and affection. As you felt confused as a child, you feel confused as an adult, so you struggle to understand romantic relationships and behave healthily with your partners. On one hand, you don't feel worthy of love, so you distance yourself from them. On the other hand, you crave long-lasting relationships. You hurt so much as a child that you find it hard to trust others and don't want to be hurt again, so you feel mixed emotions about intimate relationships. For example, if you have a disorganized attachment style, you might feel and express love and appreciation for your partner for some time, then doubt their commitment and push them away.

WORKBOOK EXERCISES

It's time to put into practice what you've just learned! Try the following activities with your partner and discuss what you've discovered and what has surprised you the most.

Mapping Your Relationship Timeline

Let's start with reflecting on your relationship and how well you know your partner. Before doing any activity discussed in this book, answer the following questions. If you want, you can do the activity together by writing down your answers on a piece of paper and comparing them. This way, you enhance self-awareness and understand how well you know each other. After years of being together, you might believe you know and remember everything about each other, but is it true? Test yourself!

- When is your partner's birthday?
- Where were they born?
- Name their two closest friends.
- What is their favorite meal?
- What makes them feel competent?
- Name something they are currently stressed about.
- Name something they are insecure about.
- What are their hobbies?
- What is their favorite local restaurant?
- What do they do to relax?
- What is their favorite way to spend an evening?
- What is their favorite dessert?
- What is their favorite movie?
- What is their greatest fear?
- What is their biggest pet peeve?
- Do they want children? If so, how many?
- What has been their biggest accomplishment?

- What would their ideal date night include?
- What would they buy if they found $50?
- What is their dream vacation?
- What is a subject they are passionate about?
- What is their favorite way to spend time with you and show you they love you?
- What makes them feel loved?
- What do they like most about themselves?

After completing the above activity, create a visual timeline of your relationship, including all the significant events, from the most positive to the most negative, milestones, and whatever you consider important. To make the exercise more interesting and productive, use colors or symbols to represent different emotions or themes associated with each event. Once you've drawn the timeline, look at it and identify patterns in your relationship and growth areas or things you know you can improve as a couple.

Discovering Your Attachment Style

Discover your attachment style to understand your relationship with your primary caregiver and how it influences your present connection with your lifelong companion. Try the following quiz: www.attachmentproject.com/attachment-style-quiz. You'll have to answer a series of questions concerning your primary caregiver, which is usually your mother, your secondary caregiver, which is probably your father, and your partner. When answering, you'll have to choose how much you identify yourself with the sentences presented in the quiz on a scale from 0 to 7, where 0 stands for "I strongly disagree with this affirmation" and 7 stands for "I strongly agree with this affirmation."

After completing the quiz, discuss the results with your partner openly. Don't focus on judging them or helping them "fix" their attachment style but on enhancing empathy and understanding between each other. Try to put yourself in their shoes and think about how their attachment style reflects in their daily behaviors and words.

Rediscovery Through Storytelling

After discovering your attachment style, increase your connection with each other by sharing a story from your relationship when you felt a particularly strong connection or managed to overcome a challenge together. Don't just tell your story, but analyze the situation considering what you've just learned about your attachment style: How did it influence your actions and choices? Could you have behaved differently, maybe more productively? The more you open up to your partner, the more you deepen your connection, so don't be afraid of telling the truth and expressing your opinion on life events that concern both. In the beginning, you might feel uncomfortable, but then, you'll notice the incredible effects of this activity and enhance your empathy and connection.

Understanding the roots of your relationship and each other's attachment styles is a critical first step in your journey toward mutual growth. It's also a fundamental factor in improving verbal and nonverbal communication, which we'll discuss in the next chapter.

WEEK 2: ENHANCING COMMUNICATION

> *The biggest problem in communication is the illusion that it has taken place.*
>
> — WILLIAM H. WHYTE

In the first years of your relationship, you've probably sacrificed something you enjoyed to show your partner your commitment and effort in building a strong connection. For example, you might have given up your favorite food because you thought they didn't like it, and you didn't want to eat different meals for dinner. After some time, you might have realized that all your effort was useless because your partner doesn't actually dislike your favorite food—they just prefer eating something else for dinner but are willing to eat it for lunch or on other occasions.

This is a clear example of ineffective communication in couples and is pretty common. After years of being together, you might realize you misunderstood your partner's ideas, needs, and wants and discover that they're different from what you expected. We all have those revealing, random conversations that suddenly change our perception of our partners and make us more aware of their true selves. How can we avoid such situations and make sure that we're always up-to-date with their needs and wants? In this chapter, we'll learn the significance of effective communication and how to put it into practice to deepen our connection with our partners.

EXPLORING THE IMPORTANCE OF EFFECTIVE COMMUNICATION

As the quote at the beginning of this chapter suggests, communication is much more complicated than you would expect. We all tend to believe that words are easy to understand and that others will successfully interpret our message even if we don't use the exact sentences we had in mind. We communicate so much every day that we take this action for granted and believe it's the simplest thing in the world. Due to these misconceptions, we tend to overlook the significance of communication and how verbal and nonverbal language impact our interactions with others.

Communication is the act of transferring information from one individual—the sender—to another—the recipient. The sender is responsible for conveying a clear, concise message that can be easily interpreted, while the recipient is responsible for analyzing the message correctly and responding appropriately. To send and receive a message effectively, both the sender and recipient must pay attention to verbal and non-verbal communication, which correspond to the words and body language used. If the sender conveys mixed messages and their words don't match their body language, the recipient is more likely to misunderstand or misinterpret their messages. At the same time, if the recipient isn't fully involved in the conversation or is distracted, they're more likely to provide inappropriate answers. This means that even using your smartphone or thinking about something else while talking to your partner might hinder your ability to interpret their words correctly.

That's why there's a clear distinction between poor and effective communication: In the first case, you often misinterpret or misunderstand the messages you receive, or you struggle to express yourself properly, while in the second case, you honestly talk about your feelings and thoughts and convey messages that are easy to interpret. Let's look at an example. Imagine being upset about a behavior your partner engaged in. They notice something is wrong, so they ask you if everything's okay, and you answer something like, "Yes, of course." But then, you don't maintain eye contact while talking to them and appear distant. This is how poor communication works. If you effectively communicate your emotions and thoughts, when your partner asks you if something's wrong, you answer something like, "Actually, yes, I'm a bit upset because of something you did recently, and I'd like to discuss it with you." This way, you clearly express your emotions and avoid causing any misinterpretation by clarifying why you feel upset.

The significance of effective communication is beyond measure because it's paramount for all relationships, especially romantic ones. If you and your partner effectively communicate with each other, you enhance respect, intimacy, and understanding because you take the time to put yourselves in each other's shoes and become aware of your inner selves. In addition, you know each other better and on a deeper level as you express yourselves properly and have a clear idea of how each other feels. Thanks to effective communication, you also avoid guesswork, which is often a cause of conflict: You don't guess how your partner feels or what they want from you, but you ask them, and they do the same with you. Moreover, you clearly express your thoughts and emotions, thus making your partner understand when you need help and how they can support you during challenging times. Finally, effective communication boosts your mood and makes you feel appreciated and loved because you feel free to talk about everything. As you can see, it helps you build your relationship and make it last forever.

But why is effective communication difficult to achieve? Well, many partners believe that not communicating is better than communicating, so they simply avoid difficult or hot topics that might hinder their relationship. When something bad happens, they convince themselves that their negative emotions and thoughts will go away by themselves, so there's no need to talk about them. At the same time, they believe that diving deeper into their struggles within the couple will only make things worse. Another common pitfall involves focusing on being right rather than finding an effective solution for both. In fact, many partners are so focused on "winning" arguments that they don't even pay attention to what their loved ones say and think, thus causing more heated conflicts and misunderstandings.

In addition, many people tend to get defensive or shut down during difficult conversations, thus stopping to listen to their partners or refusing to talk. Arguably, the most common pitfall is believing that our significant others can read our minds. After years of being together, we think they know us so well that we don't need to explain ourselves or clarify what we want from them. However, effective communication also involves clarifying our needs and wants whenever necessary to avoid misunderstandings. Therefore, we can't expect our partners to know what we want from them but tell them.

If you want to improve your communication skills, the first step is to start listening instead of hearing. When you listen, you actively participate in the conversation with your partner, are fully present and put effort into listening to their words. When you hear, you passively listen to them without focusing on the conversation, so you're not fully present. To practice effective communication, listen to your partner carefully; in particular, practice active listening to build a strong and deep connection with them. In the next section, you'll discover how to do it.

PRACTICAL COMMUNICATION TIPS

To practice active listening, you need to be fully present in the here and now and direct your attention to your partner when they talk to you. This involves using body language and words to show them you're interested in what they want to say and are listening to them: Maintain eye contact, turn your body toward them, and use sentences like "Hmm" or "I understand." If you want to be fully present, you must also eliminate all the distractions within and outside you, which means that you must stop daydreaming or thinking about your problems, and you must put your smartphone away.

When talking to others, we all tend to think about what to say next while the speaker is talking, but this behavior prevents us from fully listening to their words. Therefore, focus on their words and start thinking about an appropriate answer after they've finished their speech. Don't be afraid of silence or breaks, as they're an important part of communication, too. When thinking about the best answer, withhold judgment, be patient, and reflect on what you've just heard. If you feel like you didn't grasp the meaning of your partner's words, try to paraphrase or summarize what they just said. Then, ask open-ended questions to encourage them to keep talking and deeply understand their thoughts and emotions.

Another important factor in understanding your partner and conveying the right message is nonverbal communication, which is also a fundamental element of active listening. Nonverbal communication is everything you communicate not with your words but with your body. It includes touch, body language, eye contact, facial expressions, posture, voice, and gestures. The way you move your body and use your voice has the power to convey different messages and influences your verbal communication: If they don't match, the recipient will likely become suspicious and understand that something's wrong with what you're telling them.

To practice effective communication, you must become aware of your and your partner's nonverbal communication. When talking to them, pay attention to your posture and how you make eye contact, and try to control your facial expressions and adjust them according to the message you want to convey. Then, associate specific body language with particular emotions: How do you move your body when you feel happy, relaxed, stressed, overwhelmed, and so on? The more you become aware of your body language, the more you manage to interpret it correctly in your partner.

Another practical tip involves becoming more assertive. Assertiveness is a communication style that allows you to stand up for yourself and express your thoughts and emotions clearly without judging others or imposing your point of view. This means that you don't behave either too passively, thus not making your voice heard, or too aggressively, thus making others feel attacked. How can you become more assertive? Start with analyzing your feelings and understanding what makes you feel good and bad.

Before starting a conversation with your partner, make sure to be calm and think about what you want from them and why. Don't let negative emotions overwhelm you and dictate your reactions but remember that the calmer you are, the smoother the conversation will go.

Then, use I-statements that allow you to express your opinion without hurting your partner. No matter what you want to tell them, start with "I" and label your emotions. Next, explain why you feel that way and use words like "I need you to" or "I want you to" to clearly express what you want from your partner. Imagine that you're angry because they always come back home late for work and prioritize their job over your relationship. First, reflect on your emotions and understand if you truly feel angry or maybe you feel something different, like disappointment or resentfulness. Then, stay calm and use a sentence similar to this one: "I feel upset when you come back home late because I think you prioritize your work over our relationship. I need you to change this situation in some way." Make sure to emphasize that this sentence represents your opinion and not the reality so that your partner doesn't feel attacked and is more likely to respond calmly. Then, propose to find a solution together without imposing your point of view or forcing your partner to do something in particular.

To make sure you enhance your communication gradually but regularly, schedule regular check-ins to keep track of your emotions and discuss them together. This way, you make sure that small issues don't get bigger, and you tackle them as soon as they arise.

THE LANGUAGES OF LOVE

In the previous chapter, you discovered the importance of attachment theory in understanding your and your partner's attachment style to improve your relationship. A concept linked with attachment theory that has become more and more popular in the last decades is "love languages." In 1992, author Gary Chapman published his famous book *The 5 Love Languages*, where he described the main love languages we use to express and receive love (Bedosky, 2024). He believed that we express and receive love in five different ways: gift-giving, words of affirmation, quality time, physical touch, and acts of service. Although we use all of them, we tend to prefer one over the others and stick to it in our romantic relationships. Like the attachment style, our love language is also learned and developed during childhood and influenced by our relationship with our parents. If they expressed love toward us through gift-giving, we're more likely to use the same love language with our partners. As you might guess, understanding your and your partner's love language is essential in deepening your connection and enhancing intimacy.

Let's look at the five love languages in detail. If you express love through gift-giving, you enjoy giving and receiving gifts from your partner. This doesn't mean that you spend a lot of money buying things for them but that you dedicate time and effort to finding the perfect gift, even if it's something simple and cheap. Words of affirmation involve using words to express your love, appreciation, and admiration for your partner: You're their wild-eyed fanatic who supports and encourages them to achieve their goals, and you always have kind words for them. You tend to repeat to them how much you love them and appreciate everything they do for you. The love language of quality time is easy to understand: You enjoy spending quality time with your partner and want them to do the same with you. Therefore, you always try to set aside some time for a deep conversation or a meaningful activity to practice together, even if it's just having dinner. You don't need your partner to remind you how much they love you every day because you prefer that they show it to you.

If your love language is physical touch, you enjoy staying physically close to your partner and appreciate hugs and kisses on all occasions. You like cuddling on the couch while watching a movie or holding hands while going for a walk. If you're upset or have a bad day, you know that a hug is enough to cheer you up. Last but not least, if your love language is acts of service, you like doing practical things for your partner to ease their workload and stress and help them feel relaxed. You don't need to express your love through words because you show it to them by washing the dishes for them, running errands at their place, or cooking a delicious meal. When you notice they have a tough day, you let them relax on the couch while you clean the house or prepare dinner because you think that gestures are fundamental for the well-being of your relationship. In fact, you appreciate it when your partner does things for you as you do for them.

WORKBOOK EXERCISES

Are you ready to test your communication skills and discover your and your partner's love language? Try the following activities together.

Committing to Daily "Heart-to-Heart" Talks

Regular communication is essential for your relationship, so foster it each day! Set aside a few minutes every day to have an open and uninterrupted conversation with your significant other about their work, feelings, or whatever has happened recently. Make sure to schedule your conversation so that you never forget about it and look forward to it. Moreover, keep in mind that you don't need to revolutionize your routine and spend one or two hours sitting on the couch, talking about your deepest feelings, but you just need to be open and honest for a few minutes (10 or 15 are already enough).

In addition, create a safe space where you both feel comfortable sharing openly without fearing judgment or rejection by following the SAFER strategy.

- **Set a positive tone:** When starting a conversation, don't allow negativity to set the tone by complaining about your problems or how your partner doesn't meet your needs, but use positive and uplifting language. Remember that they deserve the best of you—no matter how tough your day was.
- **Avoid absolute language:** When you're upset, you might be used to using absolute language and tell your partner how they *always* fail to do something or *never* manage to satisfy you. Words like "always" and "never" don't correspond to reality and only make your partner react defensively, so avoid them. Instead, recognize that they do something nice for you every now and then.
- **Focus on listening:** Avoid focusing on your point of view or thinking that you're right while your partner is wrong. In addition, don't think about what to say next or how to prove your ideas. Instead, remember that the most effective way of communicating is listening: The more deeply you listen to your partner, the more you understand them and can respond appropriately to their needs and wants.

- **Emotions:** Become aware of your emotions and choose wisely before saying anything, as you might hurt your partner and cause an unnecessary conflict. Remember that they have feelings, too, and they might have different opinions on the same topic, so be empathetic and understanding.
- **Respect:** Respect each other's boundaries, even in the most complicated situations. Sometimes, you might feel the need to vent or know what your partner is feeling while they're not emotionally available and need time alone to reflect. Respect their point of view and simply give them space.

Discovering and Sharing Love Languages

Are you curious to know your love language and your partner's? Try the following online quiz: 5lovelanguages.com/quizzes/love-language. Share your results and answer this question: How can you use the newly acquired information about your partner's love language to better meet their emotional needs?

Identifying and Supporting Each Other's Needs and Wishes

This activity might be a bit more complicated than the previous two because it requires being honest with each other, even if it involves telling hard truths. Each of you must take a piece of paper and write down the needs and wishes you don't think are met or could be improved in your relationship. For example, you might note that your partner doesn't listen to you as deeply as you would like, or they don't like participating in certain activities you truly enjoy. After writing down your unmet needs, discuss them together. You might both be disappointed or surprised by your partner's thoughts and need some time to elaborate on them. Take all the time you need to discuss your unmet needs openly, honestly, and without judgment. Finally, brainstorm ways to support each other in meeting your needs and improving your relationship.

In this chapter, you learned how effective communication lays the groundwork for expressing and receiving appreciation in ways that resonate deeply. In the next one, you'll dive deep into the art of appreciation and ways to understand and practice it in your daily life. You'll also learn how it's a natural and powerful extension of effective communication that further solidifies the bond between you and your partner.

WEEK 3: APPRECIATING YOUR PARTNER

 Gratitude is not only the greatest of virtues but the parent of all others.

— MARCUS TULLIUS CICERO

Gratitude isn't only an important quality we should all possess but also essential to build a loving and respectful relationship with our partners. After years of being together, it's normal to forget to be grateful for everything our loved ones do for us. After all, they've done the same things again and again: Cooking for us, filling our glass of water every day, going grocery shopping when we don't have time, or taking a day off to spend more time with us. It all seems so predictable that we don't feel the need to thank them for their actions. However, gratitude is paramount for long-lasting relationships and must be cultivated for our whole lives. That's why, in the next sections, we'll dig deeper into this concept and discuss practical strategies to become more grateful in our daily lives.

THE SCIENCE BEHIND

Gratitude is a positive emotional response that we perceive when we give or receive a benefit from someone (Chowdhury, 2019). In other words, we feel grateful when someone does something nice for us or when we do something nice for someone else. But why should we want to enhance gratitude in our lives? Many scientists have confirmed its benefits for our mental and physical health through extensive research (Chowdhury, 2019). For example, they discovered that it increases feelings of contentment and pleasure, thus making us feel happier. In turn, the more we feel happy, the more we improve our relationships with ourselves and others. This means that gratitude allows us to become more aware of our inner selves and have more positive interactions with the people around us. This happens because we fill our minds with positive emotions that generate more positive emotions, thus creating a virtuous circle of good vibes and spreading joy everywhere.

Gratitude not only brings us happiness but also makes us feel better physically by enhancing the quality of our sleep, producing less stress, and building emotional awareness. Studies confirm that gratitude positively correlates with more energy, vitality, and enthusiasm to work harder (Chowdhury, 2019). Therefore, the more grateful we feel, the more energetic we become. Moreover, gratitude helps us build stronger and deeper connections even outside our personal lives and in our workplace, as it makes us more productive, responsible, and efficient.

But how can gratitude be so powerful? It impacts our brain in many different ways: It releases toxic emotions through the limbic system, which is responsible for our ability to regulate our emotions. It activates when we feel grateful and helps us over-come negative feelings and recover more rapidly from stressful events. Moreover, gratitude enhances our physical well-being by reducing pain symptoms and making us more willing to cooperate during treatments. This is because feelings of gratitude release dopamine and serotonin, which are two neurotransmitters responsible for positive emotions: The more grateful we feel, the more energetic and motivated we become (Chowdhury, 2019).

If that's not enough, gratitude improves our mental health by helping us manage stress effectively and reducing symptoms of anxiety and depression. A study has found that participants who felt grateful showed lower levels of cortisol (which is responsible for feelings associated with stress), better cardiac functioning, and enhanced resilience to negative experiences and setbacks. If we learn to appreciate all the small things that make our lives better, we automatically rewire our brains to focus on the positive aspects and deal with negative circumstances with a renewed, more positive perspective. An evident consequence of managing stress more effectively is reducing symptoms of anxiety and depression. Thanks to gratitude, we better regulate our prefrontal cortex, which is responsible for managing negative emotions. By feeling grateful, we automatically reduce negative feelings, become more empathetic, and develop a positive mindset (Chowdhury, 2019).

Were you aware of all the incredible effects gratitude has on our brains? I guess not, like many of us. This fundamental positive emotional state has the power to rewire our brains and change the neural structures inside of them to make us feel happier and have more positive emotions. Some scientists have also suggested that by practicing gratitude in our daily lives, we can alter the way we see ourselves and the world around us (Chowdhury, 2019).

THE IMPORTANCE OF GRATITUDE

The positive impact of gratitude on our lives doesn't stop here: Scientists have found that it also increases relationship commitment and satisfaction. By being grateful toward each other, couples not only enhance their positive emotions in the moment but are also more likely to face stress and challenges more easily in the long term. In other words, gratitude leaves a long-lasting mark in romantic relationships. Partners are more resilient to external and internal stressors, thus meaning that they respond appropriately to negative thoughts and emotions and daily stressful situations or obstacles that come from work, personal life, and responsibilities (Forrest, 2022).

One study, in particular, analyzed the effect of expressed and perceived gratitude on couples to understand the importance of using words and gestures to show appreciation and feeling appreciated and loved by partners. Couples were examined for 15 months, during which they had to regularly rate their relationship satisfaction based on conflict resolution, expressed and perceived gratitude, and levels of financial strain. In addition, couples also had to identify their levels of stability, which involves the possibility of breaking up and confidence in the future (Forrest, 2022).

Findings showed that those who perceived gratitude—thus feeling loved and appreciated—felt more satisfied with their relationship, felt greater confidence in their future, and reported fewer negative thoughts and arguments about breaking up. Moreover, perceived gratitude had a "protective effect" on the couple both in the short and long term: Even when they experienced financial hardship or struggled to solve conflicts effectively, feelings of love and appreciation saved their levels of relationship satisfaction and confidence. Therefore, perceived gratitude has the power to maintain a healthy and positive relationship in the long run and even during challenging periods of financial strain or decreased effective communication (Forrest, 2022).

This is a fundamental result because not all couples are good at communicating effectively, especially during tough times, so they risk straining their relationship. However, feeling loved and appreciated can help them feel closer to their partners and overcome all obstacles. As for the expressed gratitude, although it increases relationship satisfaction, stability, and confidence, it doesn't produce the "protective effect" perceived gratitude does (Forrest, 2022). Consequently, making your partner feel loved and appreciated is more important than simply saying "thank you."

Another study investigated the link between expressing gratitude and staying together and achieved incredible results: Researchers discovered that gratitude was an essential factor in predicting couples who would stay together or break up after nine months. The more partners expressed gratitude toward each other, the more likely they were to keep being in their relationship. In addition, studies found that expressing gratitude had incredibly positive effects not only for the couples as a whole but also for the partners who expressed gratitude daily. In fact, they enhanced their physical and emotional well-being by reducing inflammation, increasing sleep quality, and diminishing symptoms of depression. Such findings prove that taking care of ourselves is important for our mental and physical health, but focusing on and helping others also improves our lives (*What Makes a Good Relationship? Gratitude, Say Experts.*, 2022).

Being grateful toward our partners and the amazing things that happen every day has a huge impact on our relationships and produces a positive loop that makes us feel happier and happier. The more we feel grateful, the more positive emotions we experience, and the more we see the world from a renewed perspective.

Keep in mind that to express gratitude, you mustn't only thank all the people and things around you but also yourself: Dedicate a few seconds every day to be grateful for what you do at work, to improve your relationship, and to take care of your mental and physical health, even if it's a small gesture.

WAYS TO BE GRATEFUL

Making your partner feel loved and appreciated and being grateful varies depending on your and their character, so there's no unique way of expressing gratitude. As you learned in the previous chapter, there are different love languages and ways to express and receive love in a relationship, so you just have to find out what you and your partner prefer and focus on it. This doesn't mean that there are no useful tips and techniques to enhance appreciation in your daily life.

You can practice gratitude by yourself through mindfulness, a gratitude journal, and reflecting on past events. Mindfulness is an ancient technique that allows you to focus on the here and now and become more grateful for all the little things that happen in your daily life. By becoming more mindful, you appreciate your life and are more compassionate toward yourself: You recognize all the effort you put into becoming a better person and partner and understand your value. To practice mindfulness, you don't need to do anything in particular except pay more attention to the things you do every day, including eating and walking. Mindful eating involves focusing on the meal you're consuming through all your senses, thus paying attention to how it looks, tastes, and smells, its texture, and the sounds you hear while eating it. Mindful walking is based on focusing on the way you walk, how your body moves, and everything around you. Like many of us, you might have walked the same streets every day for years without identifying all the details and beautiful aspects of the environment. Thanks to mindful walking, you become aware of them and appreciate your life more.

To keep a gratitude journal, you just have to write down the things you're grateful for each day or week. Remember that it mustn't become a daily chore but a pleasant activity that helps you express gratitude, so don't do it every day if you notice the exercise becomes monotonous and doesn't improve your mood. If you want, you can keep a weekly gratitude journal where you record your positive feelings at the end of each week. The best part of the day to write your journal is before bedtime because you can reflect on the things that happened throughout the day and how they made you feel.

Being grateful for the good things in your life is easy, while being for the bad ones might be hard, but it's an important activity that allows you to know yourself and learn life lessons. Therefore, take some time to reflect on past events, especially the ones that made you feel bad or were characterized by poor choices and impulses, like lashing out at your best friend, a missed career opportunity, or a poor financial decision. Choose two or three events and reflect on the positive effects they had on your life, relationships, and skills. I'm sure that you'll discover that you've learned a lot from them and grown as an individual.

In addition to practicing gratitude by yourself, you can also do it with your partner. The first thing that probably comes to your mind when thinking about being more grateful is saying "Thank you" more often, which is certainly a good tip. However, you can do much more than that. For example, you can say "Thank you" not only for the things your partner does for you but also for who they are. After being together for some time, you might take their personality and unique traits for granted and not feel the need to appreciate them as you did during the first years. But they're still important and define the person you've decided to spend your whole life with, so be grateful for them. Tell your partner how grateful you are for them being kind, compassionate, clever, or organized.

To make them feel loved and appreciated, you can also be more present in their life and praise them in front of other people, like friends and family members. Small gestures like a thoughtful message or a rapid call out of the blue improve your partner's mood and make them feel loved and cared for because they know you are thinking about them. This is also valid when you praise them publicly, as they understand that you love them for who they are, not only in the comfort of your house and when you're alone but also when talking with loved ones and important people in your life. Therefore, they feel even more appreciated and important.

WORKBOOK EXERCISES

The above ways to be grateful are tips you can put into practice in your daily life, but you can also do something more to enhance gratitude in your relationship. Try the activities below with your partner and see the benefits of gratitude for yourself!

Writing and Exchanging Letters of Appreciation

Once a week, dedicate some time to writing and exchanging letters of appreciation where you record all the things you're grateful for in your relationship, like fond memories, nice gestures, or specific qualities. If you don't know where to start, think about your week and how your partner made it better. After writing your letters, exchange them during a quiet, intimate time to fully absorb the words of the other.

Creating a Gratitude Jar

If you don't feel comfortable writing letters, you can try something simpler and quicker: the gratitude jar. In the previous sections, you learned the importance of keeping a gratitude journal and how to do it in your daily life. Creating a gratitude jar is not so different, but it allows you to develop a deeper connection with your partner, as you must complete this activity together. First, find an old jar you don't use and put it somewhere in your house where you can easily reach it. Then, put some pieces of paper and a pen close to it so that they're always there for you. Finally, simply write a gratitude note and put it in the jar. Feel free to repeat this activity as many times as you want throughout the day and each time you think about what you're grateful for. You don't need to write long sentences but things like, "I'm thankful for my job because it makes me grow professionally" or "I'm grateful for my partner who prepared dinner for me."

To make the activity more effective, read your gratitude notes every few days or once a week to become aware of what you're thankful for and share your thoughts and emotions. In addition, you can use the gratitude notes in times of need. In fact, you might have a particularly busy week or a tough day and struggle to be grateful for anything in your life: Your boss complains about something you did, your partner is upset, or your friends are too busy to talk to you. In such cases, you don't need to despair—use your gratitude jar instead! Pick up one or two notes from the jar and simply read them to remind you of all the things you were grateful for until a day or week ago. This way, you manage to look at the big picture and overcome the negative emotions you're feeling at that specific moment. Keep in mind that creating a gratitude jar is effective if you put effort into it, but don't force yourself to find something to be grateful for each day; so don't stress about writing a gratitude note each day, but be spontaneous.

Planning an Appreciation Day

Do you remember the five love languages you learned about in the previous chapter? Well, you can use them to plan an appreciation day. Dedicate one day every once in a while to showing appreciation toward each other through your love languages. For example, if you know that your partner's love language is quality time, you take a day off and organize a day trip somewhere special to spend some time in nature together without distractions like work or technological devices. This way, you tailor your appreciation in a way that deeply resonates with them, thus making them feel even more loved and appreciated and fostering a profound connection. Remember to schedule your appreciation day to make sure you celebrate it, and don't accidentally schedule other, less important activities on the same day.

During the third week of your journey toward mutual growth, you learned that acts of appreciation not only enrich the emotional landscape of your relationship but also lay a fertile ground for confidence and trust toward each other to flourish. The next natural step in strengthening your bond is focusing on improving trust, which is deeply interconnected with gratitude.

WEEK 4: IMPROVING TRUST

 Trust is the glue of life. It's the most essential ingredient in effective communication. It's the foundational principle that holds all relationships.

— STEPHEN R. COVEY

Trust is the fundamental element that ensures effective communication and enhanced gratitude within the couple. If you don't trust each other, you risk provoking useless arguments and misunderstandings and not feeling grateful for the amazing person your partner is. Imagine that one of your friends discovers that your significant other had a meeting with one of their exes and didn't tell you. If you don't trust them, you might panic, believe that they're cheating on you, and cause a heated argument, thus straining your relationship. How can you trust your partner? In this chapter, you'll learn the essential role trust plays in your relationship, the consequences of breaking it, and strategies to strengthen it. Then, you'll find practical activities to try with your partner to enhance trust together.

THE GLASS THAT PROTECTS RELATIONSHIPS

Trust is the foundation of all healthy relationships, as they can't last long without it. If you trust your partner, you rely on them and are convinced that they will never hurt you in any way. The concept of trust is strictly connected with vulnerability because when you trust, you feel comfortable with your authentic self and know you can express all your emotions and thoughts without being hurt. In other words, you know you can show your vulnerability, flaws, and shortcomings without losing your partner. If your relationship is based on trust, you notice it because you feel comfortable talking to each other about everything—even the hottest topics—you're not afraid of admitting mistakes, you both feel confident in expressing your thoughts and emotions, and you show your true selves to each other without hesitation.

Trust matters in all romantic relationships because it makes you feel safe and secure, enhances your communication with each other, helps you overcome obstacles more easily, and you feel confident in giving each other space to achieve your personal goals and do activities you enjoy. In general, improving trust allows you to get closer to each other, have fewer conflicts, and feel more positive emotions in the relationship. You know you can face all challenges together because you'll be there for each other and do whatever you can to save your relationship. If you think about it, the fact that you're reading this book together and undertaking your journey toward mutual growth is a good sign of trust and commitment toward each other. In addition, trusting not only helps you deepen your connection but also gives you enough space to pursue personal goals. In fact, you know you'll always balance your needs and prioritize your relationship, so you trust each other that you won't break up because of personal aspirations.

Lack of trust is one of the main reasons why couples break up, so you must pay attention to and value it in your daily life. Reflect on your situation for a few seconds: Where are you right now as far as trust is concerned? Do you believe you should improve? Is trust broken between you? Take a few seconds to recall the first months and years of your relationship and how you built trust together. You'll probably remember how much time you spent believing in each other and feeling free to be vulnerable and express your authentic selves. In fact, trust is built over years and requires a lot of time, effort, and patience. At the same time, it can be easily broken due to a fatal mistake that makes your partner doubt your honesty and commitment to the relationship. For these reasons, you must be careful not to break the glass that protects your connection.

WHEN THE GLASS BREAKS

What happens when the glass breaks? Well, it can have terrible consequences for your relationship. In particular, broken trust produces important emotional, psychological, and physical effects. The most common emotional reactions involve anxiety, resentment, a sense of betrayal, anger, confusion, and sadness. If you don't trust your partner anymore, you might feel hurt and lose trust not only in them but also in yourself and the rest of the world. You might be so surprised by their actions that you doubt everything you see and hear. In addition, you might become withdrawn and avoid social interactions, even with people whom you've trusted for all your life. Consequently, you might experience depression and feel lonely, vulnerable, and like you're not in control of your life anymore.

When trust is broken, many people blame themselves and believe that they're not good enough for their partners, thus hindering their mental health, self-esteem, and self-confidence. From a psychological perspective, you might start overthinking and struggle with negative thoughts because you focus on the bad things that happen to you and all your flaws and shortcomings. You believe that your partner betrayed your trust for a specific reason that involves your incompetence and inability to give them what they want and need in a relationship. This way, you enter a vicious circle that makes you feel worse and more isolated. All these emotional and psychological effects have repercussions on your physical health, too, as you might have difficulty sleeping due to all your negative thoughts or have headaches or nausea. A breach of trust is undoubtedly a traumatic event that changes your perspective on the world, the people around you, and your-self, thus making you feel less secure and safe.

The reasons why trust is broken are multifaceted, but there are some common behaviors that make partners feel less secure and safe in their relationships. For example, if your loved one tells lies or omits the truth, you might immediately change the way you look at and interact with them. It's normal to avoid discussing certain topics or hiding certain flaws at the beginning of a rela-tionship, as we all want to convince our future partners that we're perfect for them. But if lies continue, then it's not healthy, and you risk straining your relationship because they'll come back to you sooner or later, and you'll have to face consequences. Another common way of breaking trust is keeping secrets, which is not absolutely bad *per se*. If your partner is discreet, they might feel comfortable keeping some things for themself, and there's nothing wrong about it. However, they should tell you everything that could impact the image you have of them and your relation-ship. Another typical behavior is breaking promises, which always hurts partners. Keeping your promises isn't always easy, so you might break one or two every once in a while—after all, you can't predict the future precisely. However, repeatedly breaking promises slowly impacts trust and decreases the quality of your relationship.

In addition to these evident, generic behaviors, trust can be broken in your daily life through apparently harmless actions you might engage in. For instance, being late most of the time can hurt your partner, as they feel like they can't count on you. The same is true when you don't listen to them because they believe you don't love them enough to pay attention to their words and be there for them. In the long term, they might decide to stop talking to you. Trust is also broken when you don't express your feelings in your daily life, which is not different from keeping secrets or omitting the truth: If you don't show your emotions, your partner doesn't know how you feel, so they get confused and struggle to understand you. They might see you as unreliable also when you don't do your share of tasks and responsibilities, like house chores, because they believe they can't count on you for practical, daily support. These are just some of the daily actions you might engage in that might hinder trust in your relationship.

STRENGTHENING THE GLASS

Have you or your partner ever engaged in some of the above behaviors? Probably yes, as happens to many couples. However, there's nothing to worry about because you can improve your relationship and restore trust by committing to becoming more reliable and being more present for each other. The first step to strengthening the delicate glass of trust involves taking responsibility for your actions. When you break promises, tell lies, or keep secrets, you might convince yourself that it's not your fault, and you are forced to act like that for external reasons that don't depend on you. However, you have control over the things you say and do, so you must take responsibility for them. Instead of saying something like, "I didn't want to tell you this thing because I didn't want to make you angry or sad," try saying something like, "I deliberately chose to omit the truth to avoid making you feel negative emotions." Can you see the difference? I guess so. If you get used to taking responsibility for your actions, you're more likely to avoid repeating behaviors that might break trust because you don't want to be responsible for the end of your relationship, like no one would.

If you struggle to keep your promises, you might have difficulty managing your time or predicting your future behaviors. Therefore, I suggest that when you're about to make a promise, think carefully about it and only make it if you're 100% sure you're going to keep it. Remember to consider all possible obstacles, incidents, and worst-case scenarios so that you're more realistic. You're not forced to make promises, so avoid doing it if you know you can't keep them. The secret to strengthening trust in your relationship is to be transparent and honest all the time. The more you keep the truth to yourself, the more you risk straining your connection with your partner. You might feel uncomfortable being completely honest, but it's normal because we all tend to believe that hiding the truth is better than hurting our loved ones with a harsh reality. Just keep in mind that you don't hurt them if you show your true self—you deepen your relationship.

In particular, developing trust helps you make deposits in your relationship's emotional bank account, a concept that has been coined by the famous author Steven Covey and isn't different from a typical personal bank account. While the latter allows you to make deposits and withdrawals of money, the emotional bank account is based on the idea of giving and receiving emotional support. The more deposits you make, the more positive emotions you introduce in your relationship. Conversely, withdrawing emotional support creates anxiety, conflict, and stress. To make more deposits and improve your connection with your partner, you must build trust, which is an essential component of a wealthy emotional bank account. The more trust you develop, the richer your relationship will become (Ncube, 2023).

WORKBOOK EXERCISES

Now, it's time to get practical! Complete the following activities with your partner to increase trust toward each other.

Engaging in Trust-Building Activities

There are plenty of trust-building activities you can try with your partner, and they're all funny and exciting! Thanks to them, you can not only enhance trust in your relationship but also bring more fun to it. You find a list of some entertaining exercises below.

- **Cuddle for 10 minutes:** Set a timer to cuddle for 10 minutes a day with your partner. When you have many responsibilities and are in a relationship for some time, you might forget about little, kind gestures like cuddling. Instead of getting out of bed as soon as the alarm clock goes off or turning the lights off as soon as you touch the bed before sleeping, spend 10 minutes cuddling. This way, you increase your emotional and physical bond.
- **Try something new together:** To increase relationship satisfaction, try a new activity together. Keep in mind that it must be new for both of you, so you learn and grow together and face the learning process as a couple. Practicing the activities discussed in this book is a good way of trying something new together.

- **Complete a task together:** This activity might seem similar to the previous one, but it's not. In this case, you just have to complete a task together, like cooking or cleaning the house, and notice each other's reactions: Does one of you take over and complete the task by themself? Do you truly collaborate? Do you act as a real team? You can repeat this exercise as long as you start collaborating like a team.

- **Share a secret:** You might believe you know everything about each other, and you don't have secrets, so you can't practice this exercise. However, I'm pretty sure there are things you don't tell each other, maybe because you're too busy or they don't appear important to you, like a gaffe at work, a reaction to a particular situation, or a specific event linked with your childhood and life before getting together. Take as much time as you need to think about a secret and share it to enhance trust and know yourselves better.

- **Ask your partner to do something for you:** Saying that you want to increase trust in your relationship is easier than doing things that actually increase trust. Whenever you feel like it, ask your partner to complete a task for you. I suggest you start small, like asking them to pick up something at the supermarket, and then, gradually increase the complexity and importance of the task. Such exercise is extremely helpful to enhance trust in your daily life.

- **Eye gaze:** This exercise requires just a few minutes of your time but is incredibly helpful. To practice eye gazing, set a timer to three or five minutes and sit down facing each other, with your knees close. Close your eyes, take a few deep breaths, reopen them, and look your partner straight in the eyes. Let a few seconds pass to let go of feelings of awkwardness or discomfort, and then say something nice to each other. Allow both of you enough time to think about what to say and say it. After you've done it, keep looking each other in the eyes until the timer goes off. Finally, share your experience and discuss how this activity makes you feel.

Facilitating Trust Conversations

Take some time to reflect on a past event that tested your trust, focusing on how you got over it. It might seem a daunting task because it's hard to talk about difficult moments in your relationship, but it's paramount to create a deeper connection and trust each other more. Then, discuss feelings and concerns about trust in a constructive manner using what you've learned in Chapter 2 about effective communication, so avoid judging each other and pay attention to each other's words. If you need help starting a deep conversation about trust, use the prompts below.

- What does "trust" mean to you?
- What qualities do I embody as a good friend to you?
- Imagine yourself in one, five, or ten years: Where do you see yourself?
- How would you like me to respond when you feel upset?
- How do we take care of and protect each other around our friends and other loved ones?
- In which life areas do you trust me, and in which ones do you think you need to develop more trust (for example, secrets, work, money, etc.)?
- Do we bring enough joy and fun to our relationship, or can we do something more to feel happier?
- Do we tend to apologize? If so, how? Can we do something to improve?

- What is success for you? Do you consider it a value of yours or our relationship?

Creating a Transparency Act

A useful exercise to improve trust in your relationship involves creating a "transparency act" where you emphasize your commitment to honesty, openness, and regular check-ins to keep track of each other's emotions, thoughts, and concerns. You don't have to write a 100-page document, but sit down and write a few sentences that highlight your effort into improving your relationship. Make sure to record the specific actions you must engage in to follow your journey toward mutual growth and when you plan to do them. The more precise you are, the more effective your "transparency act" will be. To make the exercise even more useful, consider situations that might require extra transparency and openness and include step-by-step guidelines in your act. For example, incorporate instructions on how to overcome broken promises, dirty tactics, or forms of manipulation.

Trust is an essential component of all relationships and must be cultivated over the years. If you break this glass, you risk distancing yourself from your partner and hindering your connection, so put effort into making more deposits in your emotional bank account and practicing the activities you found at the end of the chapter. Establishing a foundation of trust is also critical to achieving deeper emotional intimacy. With trust as your bedrock, you're now better equipped to explore and deepen your connection by moving toward a relationship where vulnerability is not just accepted but cherished. In the next chapter, you'll discover the significance of intimacy and ways to develop it.

WEEK 5: DEEPENING INTIMACY

 Intimacy is not purely physical. It's the act of connecting with someone so deeply you feel like you can see into their soul.

— RESHALL VARSOS

When discussing intimacy, the first thing that comes to mind for all couples is physical intimacy, which is one of the fundamental elements of a healthy and positive relationship. However, that's not everything: Intimacy goes well beyond a deep connection in bed and involves vulnerability and comfort in expressing our inner selves. In this chapter, we'll unravel the true meaning of intimacy, its different types, and ways to increase it. Finally, we'll discuss practical activities that we can easily introduce into our daily lives.

WHY INTIMACY MATTERS

In the previous chapter, we discovered the connection between trust and vulnerability and learned that trusting someone means feeling free to show our authentic selves. Developing intimacy in a romantic relationship is not so different, as it implies feeling comfortable discussing our inner thoughts and emotions, even the darkest ones. If you feel intimate with your partner, you feel emotionally and physically close to them, thus experiencing a connection you can't have with anyone else. You feel free to share your thoughts and emotions and have all sorts of experiences with them. If you feel intimate, you aren't afraid of talking about your past, future, and present, but do it openly and honestly because you know your partner will listen to you and stay close to you—no matter what you say. As you might guess, trust and intimacy go hand in hand because you can't be intimate with your partner if you don't trust them with your secrets, concerns, and thoughts.

At the same time, intimacy is built over time, just like trust. Do you remember the first time you had physical contact with each other and kissed or hugged? Like many other couples, you might have felt uncomfortable and uncertain about what to do and what you wanted from each other. After some time, you've developed trust and understood how to behave, what you dislike, and what you enjoy doing. Maybe you didn't feel comfortable holding hands in public with your partner in the first few weeks or months, but then, you became intimate with them and felt at ease with it. The same is true for your thoughts and emotions, as you've probably struggled to discuss them freely with your partner because you didn't know how they could react. Now, I guess you have a precise idea of how certain words and behaviors might make your partner feel.

But does this mean that you've reached the peak of intimacy? Knowing yourselves intimately requires patience and time as you change over the years and might have different thoughts, emotions, interests, and preferences than before. That's why intimacy must always be cultivated, and you have to keep informed about what your partner wants and needs in the relationship: They might grow up and evolve as you might. For example, you might have needed them to be physically close to you during the first few months or years of your relationship, but right now, you might need them to be emotionally close to you and provide emotional support.

How can you make sure that you develop intimacy with your partner? As already mentioned, trust is a fundamental component, as it allows you to be completely free to express your thoughts and emotions without feeling judged or criticized. In addition, you must truly care for each other because that's the only reason why you seek to fulfill each other's needs and wants. However, another essential element of intimacy is self-awareness and appreciation: If you don't know and like yourself, you're less likely to build a deep connection with your partner. If you think about it, it makes sense: How can you talk about your deepest thoughts and emotions if you're the first one not to be aware of them? The more you know your inner self, the more easily you communicate it to your partner. Then, you must come to terms with your flaws and mistakes and like yourself for who you are to truly appreciate yourself and increase the chances that others do it, too.

An important element of both trust and intimacy is honesty because you can't create a deep connection with your partner if you're not honest about what you want and like. Conversely, lying might make you feel resentful, stressed, and upset as you don't manage to satisfy your needs. Even if you think that a thought or emotion is insignificant or irrelevant for your partner, tell it to them—you might find out it's more important than you imagined. The last component of intimacy is effective communication, which is strictly connected with knowing yourself: Once you become more self-aware, you have a clear idea of what you want and need and what you think and like, so you can express it more clearly. If your relationship is characterized by all the above elements, then you can say it's intimate. If you notice that you struggle to communicate or be vulnerable in front of each other, you have the power to improve intimacy.

UNDERSTANDING TYPES OF INTIMACY

Before diving deep into the strategies to enhance intimacy in your relationship, let's take a look at the different types. As mentioned at the beginning of this chapter, intimacy is much more than just physical touch and sex. In fact, there are five main types: physical, emotional, intellectual, experiential, and spiritual.

Physical intimacy is also known as sexual intimacy and involves all physical interactions that are consensual and meaningful, from hugging to intercourse. You become physically intimate with your partner every time you touch them, like when you hold hands or give them a massage, so not everything is about sex. In addition, you can have sex without intimacy or vice versa, intimacy without sex: You can feel a deep connection and closeness to your partner even if you don't have intercourse, like when you cuddle and hug, or you can have intercourse without feeling a meaningful connection with them. Physical intimacy is also an important type of intimacy in other relationships, like between friends or a parent and child. For example, two best friends can nudge each other when acting silly, or a child can lay their head on their parent's shoulder. These behaviors don't have a sexual component but are still considered forms of physical intimacy.

Emotional intimacy implies that you feel comfortable and free to express your emotions without being judged or criticized. If you feel emotionally intimate with your partner, you're not afraid to tell them when you're excited, afraid, worried, or thrilled. If you think there's a problem in the relationship, you openly discuss it because you know your significant other will listen to and support you. The secret to fostering emotional intimacy is developing a sense of safety, which means that both you and your partner feel safe to talk about everything. Examples of emotional intimacy include being comfortable discussing what you want from the relationship or past trauma that is affecting your present. Keep in mind that if you want to develop this type of intimacy, you must both be emotionally available and not be afraid of being intimate with each other.

Intellectual intimacy is similar to the emotional type but refers to your thoughts and ideas, as it involves being comfortable sharing knowledge and interests. Therefore, you have stimulating interactions about your hobbies and thoughts and are willing to challenge each other by listening to each other and considering different points of view. The key to nurturing intellectual intimacy is mutual respect because you must appreciate each other and put effort into understanding each other's perspectives. If you're intellectually intimate with your partner, you ask them for their feedback, discuss the plot of a movie respectfully, even if you disagree with each other, and talk about financial goals. You plan activities, share your favorite songs or books, and enjoy learning new things together.

If your relationship is characterized by experiential intimacy, it means that you feel comfortable sharing activities, hobbies, or interests. Therefore, you enjoy doing things together, like hiking or taking dance classes, and you feel free to be yourself. This type of intimacy is common when partners share particular interests, like comic books or board games: The more things you have in common with your significant other, the more likely you'll be to nurture experiential intimacy. Moreover, this type of bond also involves being comfortable trying new activities together, like reading a book about couple therapy, as you're doing right now. If you enjoy sharing this experience with your partner, then you have high levels of experiential intimacy in your relationship.

Finally, you might believe that spiritual intimacy is connected to religious beliefs, and that's true, but it's not all. If you feel spiritually close to your partner, you feel comfortable talking about deep thoughts and ideas, like the purpose of life or a higher power that controls the world. If you're religious, your loved one respects your point of view and lets you express your beliefs however you like. If you enjoy practicing mindfulness, they support you and might give it a try, too, to create a deeper connection. If you're spiritually intimate, you might also volunteer together or simply enjoy the sunrise. As you might guess, spiritual intimacy is a blurred concept because the word "spiritual" means different things to different people.

To foster intimacy in your relationship, remember that as you must be comfortable sharing your ideas, emotions, beliefs, hobbies, and getting physically intimate, so must your partner. If one of you feels forced to do something, then you're not deepening your connection.

WAYS TO IMPROVE INTIMACY

All types of intimacy are paramount to feeling comfortable in the relationship and not feeling judged or rejected, but the essential ones are physical and emotional intimacy. Without them, it's harder to foster the other types. That's why we'll focus on them right now and look at practical ways to develop them in your daily lives.

To nurture physical intimacy, don't focus on improving inter-course but find alternative ways to get physically close to each other, like going for a walk, sitting next to each other instead of in front of each other at the restaurant, or cuddling on the couch while watching a movie at home. The physically closer you get to each other, the more you increase physical intimacy. This also means that you must dedicate more time to touching each other. For example, don't rush out of bed in the morning or to work after having breakfast, but take just a few seconds to kiss or hug. At the same time, avoid thinking that all forms of physical touch automatically lead to sex but make sure these things are separate so you don't always expect to have intercourse after touching. In fact, sex is important in a relationship, but it's not everything, so try to improve physical intimacy in as many ways as you can think of and be patient. Take things slowly and cherish every moment of being physically close to your partner, like when you touch their hair, look them in the eyes, or rub their back. Finally, remember that communication is paramount, and you must be comfortable sharing your sexual fantasies and thoughts linked with physical intimacy.

In fact, emotional intimacy is strictly connected to physical inti-macy: If you don't feel free to express your emotions, you're less likely to develop a deep connection with your partner. To become more emotionally intimate with each other, pay more attention to your day-to-day activities and improve your routine. Start by asking your partner how they feel, what they did during the day, if they learned something new, and similar questions. Don't restrict yourself to asking the same old, close-ended questions, but go deeper and take an interest in your partner's routine. I know it might seem hard or useless in the beginning because you know exactly what you do during the day, but you might discover details you weren't aware of, thus deepening your connection. To improve your routine, you can also create rituals that help you bond with each other, like having a glass of wine at the end of the day or after finishing work. You don't have to make majestic gestures but create little, meaningful rituals that make you feel closer to each other.

Another useful tip to improve emotional intimacy is to dig up the past in ways you might not be used to. After being together for some time, you might be used to digging up old grudges during arguments to make your voice heard and prove your point. However, that only creates more conflict and resentment between you. Therefore, replace old grudges with happy memories of your first date, a dream holiday you both enjoyed or an adventure you faced together. If you struggle to think about specific events, use your social media account or pictures and videos on your phone to recall good memories. This simple activity helps you remember why you love each other and everything you've gone through together. Last but not least, never forget to appreciate your partner for who they are and what they do for you every day, as you learned in Chapter 3.

WORKBOOK EXERCISES

Are you ready to discover a new level of intimacy? Practice the following activities!

Sharing Innermost Thoughts

Like many couples, you probably keep some thoughts and feelings hidden within you. Well, it's time to talk about them openly and honestly and have a deep conversation. Make sure to avoid any form of judgment and to build a safe and positive environment where you both feel at ease discussing such delicate thoughts and emotions. If you don't know where to start, you can find a list of prompts below. As you'll notice, deep conversations can center on childhood and memories, significant life events, the meaning of love, goals and aspirations, values and principles, and the concept of relationship. These are just examples of deep topics you can face together, so try to find more considering your unique situation and background.

- What is your best and worst childhood memory?
- What was your favorite year of school?
- What is your most memorable family event?
- What events are on your bucket list?
- Would you rather spend a week in New York City or San Francisco?
- What is the best concert you've ever been to?
- Can you recall our first date?
- When did you know you loved me?
- What is your favorite memory with me?
- What do you look forward to experiencing with me?
- How often do you think a couple should argue to maintain a positive relationship?
- If it's okay to lie and break the law, when is it?
- What is an unforgivable action?
- Which is more motivating: praise or criticism?
- Do you think it's better to invest or save money?
- Do you think we divide household chores equally? If not, how do you think we should do it?

Planning Surprise Date Nights

To deepen intimacy with your partner, plan surprise date nights: Take turns to organize them and make sure that they correspond to what your partner prefers doing the most. In other words, tailor date nights to their interests and desires. The key to enhancing emotional intimacy is surprise and effort, so commit to organizing an unforgettable date night that your partner would never expect! This doesn't mean that you have to schedule a dinner at the most expensive restaurant in town or visit New York in one day, as small gestures are the most important ones. Therefore, think about what your partner enjoys and organize your date night based on that: It might be taking a long walk at night before going to bed or having a drink and snack in a local bar they like. Planning surprise date nights must be a pleasure and not a burden, so don't force yourself to organize one every week, but make sure you do at least one every one or two months. If you need ideas, use the ones below.

- Go out to dinner in a new restaurant that might interest your partner.
- Visit a small city or a part of town you've never been to.
- Go hiking.
- Have a picnic.
- Build a campfire.
- Play a board game.
- Have fun at a casino.
- Take a dance class.
- Read to each other.
- Volunteer together.

Just use your imagination and think of an activity your partner would truly enjoy!

While deepening emotional intimacy brings numerous benefits to a relationship, it also opens the door to vulnerability, which can sometimes lead to conflict. That's why learning effective conflict resolution strategies is an essential next step: Thanks to them, you manage disagreements in a way that strengthens rather than weakens your deep bond with each other.

WEEK 6: RESOLVING CONFLICT

Have you ever heard the saying, "It takes two to tango?" In a romantic relationship, everything occurs because both partners are involved and responsible for their actions—especially during a conflict. When you have an argument, it's easy to fall into the trap of considering yourself right while your partner is wrong (which probably both of you believe). What many couples struggle to think about is that both partners are right and wrong at the same time, as they're both responsible for their words and actions. Even if one of them behaved badly, they're probably not the only ones to blame, as their loved one might have inadvertently said or done something to induce such a negative behavior. If both partners recognize their responsibility in the conflict, they make the first step to resolving it peacefully.

In the next sections, we'll dive deep into this concept and discover the difference between healthy and unhealthy conflict resolution, techniques to foster the former, and how boundaries help you avoid arguments. Then, we'll look at practical activities to enhance your conflict resolution skills.

A HEALTHY CONFLICT RESOLUTION

Before discussing the difference between healthy and unhealthy conflict resolution, we must understand the meaning of conflict in romantic relationships: It's a disagreement or struggle between two people that usually involves recurrent, unresolved issues, like household chores or money management. Like many of us, you might believe that conflict is bad and must be avoided at all costs, so you might be surprised to hear about "healthy conflict resolution." However, conflicts have the power to strain or improve a relationship depending on the way you look at them and face them.

A healthy or constructive conflict involves collaborative and adaptive behaviors: You accept that you and your partner have a different point of view but work together to understand each other's point of view and reach a solution that benefits both. You don't see them as opponents in a strenuous fight but as collaborators in a team, so you try your best to listen to and understand them and value their opinion. Conversely, an unhealthy or destructive conflict is characterized by escalation and avoidance —two types of behavior that lead to more heated arguments. Escalation involves becoming aggressive and hostile to defend your point of view, while avoidance implies running away from the argument, thus avoiding it without providing clear answers to your partner. It's easy to see how constructive conflict improves the relationship and enhances empathy and understanding between you and your partner, while destructive conflict leads to more problems and unresolved issues. That's why you must foster constructive conflict to deepen your connection with your significant other.

TECHNIQUES FOR CONSTRUCTIVE CONFLICT

The first step to fostering constructive conflict in your relationship is understanding that disagreements are normal and all couples argue from time to time. Therefore, accept that conflicts arise between you and your partner and focus on the fact that you have the power to make them healthier. If you want to have a deep connection with them, you don't have to avoid all arguments and agree with them all the time but face them constructively by making your voice heard and respecting theirs. How can you do so? To start, follow the tips below.

- **Listen carefully:** When a conflict arises, it's common to let emotions control our behaviors and focus on winning the argument. Therefore, we're likely to interrupt our partners while they talk or assume we know what they're thinking or what is best for them. However, such assumptions make conflict resolution harder because they don't allow us to really listen to our partners and pay attention to their words. To enhance conflict resolution with your significant other, stop assuming. Instead, concentrate on what they want to tell you and understand their point of view. The more you know about what they want and need, the more easily you'll find a compromise.

- **Avoid making the situation worse:** If your partner behaves poorly, you might be tempted to answer by behaving even more poorly, thus letting your emotions take control of the situation. I know that it's hard to keep calm and look at the big picture during a heated argument, but you must avoid making the situation worse. Adding negativity to a difficult conversation only reduces your chances of solving the conflict peacefully, so take a few seconds before reacting and remember that negative behavior is never the solution.

- **Be direct:** Destructive ways of solving arguments involve changing topics, being condescending while hiding hostility, or sulking without explaining why. Such tactics are indirect ways of expressing anger that don't help your partner understand how you feel and what you want from them. Instead, be as direct as you can and openly express your thoughts and emotions as soon as they arise to avoid misunderstandings and confusion.

- **Value your partner's ideas:** When your partner complains about something, you might react by undervaluing their words and objecting to them. By doing so, you make them believe that their ideas aren't worthwhile and risk causing more conflicts. Instead, listen carefully and consider their perspective before answering. For example, if they ask you to help them keep the house clean during the week, don't automatically say that you don't have time or are too busy with your job, but analyze the situation to find a solution that can benefit both. You can tell them something like, "I don't think I'll be able to help you every day of the week, but I can try to take a few minutes before dinner every other day."

- **Never say "never" or "always":** Some of the most used words during a conflict or even during everyday conversations are "never" and "always." It's easy to believe that certain behaviors never or always occur and tell our partners things like, "You never listen to me" or "I always have to do everything in this house!" However, such words rarely represent reality, as it's more likely that our partners listen to us or help us sometimes. In addition, saying "never" or "always" makes our loved ones feel attacked and undervalued because we don't recognize everything they do for us.

- **Change perspective:** To promote constructive conflict resolution, you must always consider and try to understand your partner's point of view, so you must put yourself in their shoes. But sometimes, it might not be enough, or you might need to look at the problem at hand more objectively. Therefore, detach yourself from the specific situation and imagine being a third party who wants the best for you and your partner. Write down your and their point of view and take a few minutes to reflect on them and see things from a different perspective. This way, you'll be more likely to be neutral and do what's best for both you and your loved one.

THE ROLE OF BOUNDARIES

One of the most common reasons why couples argue is boundaries, which are limits or lines we set for ourselves to feel comfortable and safe in a relationship. Unfortunately, we all struggle to set clear and healthy boundaries, so our partners might cross them, make us feel uncomfortable, and create conflict. For instance, they might feel at ease sharing all their financial transactions and talking about money, retirement, and financial goals, while you might find it hard to share every detail of your financial situation. If you don't set clear boundaries, your partner might keep asking you how much money you have in your bank account, what you want to do with them, and so on, thus making you feel uncomfortable. By setting clear and healthy boundaries, you clarify your position and make them understand what you consider acceptable in your relationship.

Many people struggle to set boundaries because they consider it selfish: By saying what they feel comfortable doing, they put themselves first and don't consider their partners' point of view. However, setting healthy boundaries allows all of us to clarify our expectations and build a strong and deep connection with our loved ones while respecting them and feeling safe. In other words, the whole couple benefits from setting healthy boundaries. But, in order to do so, we must first understand what boundaries are. There are five types: emotional, physical, intellectual, sexual, and financial. If you think about it, they're not so different from the types of intimacy, as boundaries and intimacy are strictly connected with each other: The healthier the boundaries, the deeper the intimacy.

Emotional boundaries involve being free to express your emotions even when they don't correspond to your partner's: Even if they're mad or sad, you don't need to be mad or sad, too. Vice versa, if you have healthy emotional boundaries, you don't expect your partner to experience the same feelings at the same time but understand that they might be happy when you're sad, and so on. Physical boundaries refer to how comfortable you feel being close to your partner. For instance, you might not be okay with kissing or holding hands in public while they do. Intellectual boundaries allow you to respect both your and your loved one's thoughts and beliefs because you're both aware that you don't have the same opinion on all topics but express different ideas. Therefore, you don't expect your partner to always back up your thoughts and vice versa. Sexual boundaries involve what you feel comfortable doing before, during, and after intercourse and are fundamental to fostering trust and intimacy in the relationship. Finally, financial boundaries refer to how comfortable you feel talking about money with your partner, and they include discussing which restaurants to go to, how to spend your income, or how to save money.

To set healthy boundaries, remember that there aren't right or wrong ones: Your partner might feel comfortable discussing all their thoughts and emotions while you might not, and that's fine. When identifying your boundaries, don't think about what your partner prefers or what's considered acceptable by the majority of people, but focus on what you want and need. You'll learn more about setting healthy boundaries in the activities below.

WORKBOOK EXERCISES

After learning some basic, useful information about healthy conflict resolution, it's time to get practical! Try the following activities together to handle arguments more effectively.

Establishing "Fair Fight" Rules

The way you enter a fight defines how it will end, so you must pay attention to what you do before starting an argument. For this reason, it's helpful to create a list of "fair fight" rules that both you and your partner must keep in mind when a conflict arises to make sure the conversation remains productive and respectful. Try to include as many details as possible so that you both have a clear idea of what is accepted and what is not accepted during an argument. If you need prompts to start your list, use the examples below. If you want, you can also include the techniques for constructive conflict discussed previously in this chapter.

- **Don't yell:** As you might guess, yelling is counterproductive because it doesn't help you make your voice heard. Conversely, it makes your loved one defensive and react negatively. If you include "don't yell" in your list, make sure to define it properly because you might consider yelling differently from your partner, depending on your background. For example, talking loudly during a conflict might be normal in some families, while others might see it as inappropriate.

- **Don't blame:** The first thing we tend to do when there's a problem is blame someone—usually not us. Finding the culprit doesn't make the situation better, so focus on finding a solution without emphasizing what your partner did wrong.

- **Don't bring up the past:** Another common unhealthy pattern is bringing up old grudges to recall all the times you were right or your loved one did something wrong. This behavior is counterproductive and doesn't allow you to concentrate on the problem at hand but might create new, more heated arguments.

- **Avoid degrading language:** You might fall into the trap of insulting or name-calling your partner and immediately regret what you said. To avoid saying something you don't want to, take a few seconds before talking and remember this fundamental "fair fight" rule.

- **Don't use force:** Threatening to use force or using it during an argument is always unacceptable. Remember that both you and your partner must feel safe and comfortable, especially during conflicts.

- **Don't talk about divorce or breakup:** Another common mistake is threatening to leave your partner to supposedly make them understand the seriousness of the problem and manipulate them to behave as you want them to. However, talking about breaking up only makes them more anxious and afraid and they might doubt your commitment to the relationship, thus breaking the fragile glass of trust.

- **Take turns:** The most effective way of facing an argument is to give each other time to express your point of view and be respectful. Therefore, take turns while speaking and avoid talking over or thinking about something else. Instead, focus on your partner's words and listen to them carefully.

- **Use time-outs:** Sometimes, the best thing to do is take a moment to calm down and continue the conversation another time. If you notice that the argument is getting heated, don't force yourself to keep arguing but accept that taking a break will help solve the problem more easily. Talk about it together and decide to take a few minutes or half an hour or continue the conversation another day. This way, you have time to reflect on what happened, look at things from a renewed perspective, and focus on what you appreciate in your partner and relationship.

- **Focus on yourself, not your partner:** It's easy to list all the things your partner does wrong and how you would do them better, but that's not how you solve a conflict peacefully. Instead, focus on yourself, your mistakes, and how you plan to improve. Talk about your emotions and thoughts and how you think you could solve the conflict. Acknowledge that if you have a problem, you have some responsibility, too, and you're willing to do whatever it takes to improve the situation.

- **Stay on topic:** Have you ever started an argument due to miscommunication issues and ended up talking about who does the laundry and goes grocery shopping every week? Well, this is an example of bringing various arguments to the same table. Even if you have different problems, just focus on one at a time so that you both have a clear idea of what you're talking about. Moreover, adding more topics to the same argument reduces the chances of finding an agreement. If you notice that one of you is digressing, stop them and help them remember why you're arguing and what the main topic is.

Boundary-Setting Activity

In the previous section, you learned about the different boundaries and the importance of setting healthy ones, but how can you do it? You can find a step-by-step guide below.

1. **Identify your boundaries:** Take inspiration from the types of boundaries you discovered in this chapter and use them to identify yours. While taking this fundamental step, remember your values and the things that are most important to you without considering your partner's preferences. Become aware of your needs and wants and how to convert them into actionable boundaries, like not holding hands in public.

2. **Communicate them:** Clearly state your boundaries by using sentences like "I feel comfortable when we do this," "I don't feel comfortable when we do this," "I don't like when you say or do these things," or "I like when you behave this way." The key to communicating is emphasizing both positive and negative behaviors so that your partner knows what you like and feel comfortable with and is more likely to repeat such actions. If you're not used to setting boundaries, start small by changing just one thing and enforcing only one limit. Then, remember that you might have kept your

feelings to yourself for a long time, but your partner might be shocked or surprised by your request and have no idea why you suddenly want to change things in the relationship. In addition, they might feel guilty or bad for having reiterated behaviors that have caused you pain for a long time, so prepare for pushback and give them time to reflect on the new boundaries and adapt to the situation.

3. **Reflect on your emotions:** When communicating your boundaries for the first time, you might feel guilty or awkward and believe that it's wrong. Accept your feelings, understand that they're normal, and acknowledge that setting boundaries makes your relationship healthier and improves your happiness and satisfaction without disrespecting your partner.

4. **Be consistent:** Communicating your boundaries once won't probably be enough, as your partner will need you to repeat them again and again, so make sure to be consistent. Whenever they make you feel uncomfortable, state your boundary kindly and enforce consequences. Keep your boundaries in mind and act as soon as your loved one crosses them to clarify your point of view further and ensure they remember it.

After reflecting on and communicating your boundaries, discuss ways in which they can be respected and integrated into your daily lives to prevent future conflicts. Make sure that you have an open, clear, and honest conversation with your partner and respect each other's perspective.

In this chapter, you discovered essential techniques to enhance your conflict resolution techniques and avoid unnecessary arguments. However, at the heart of effective conflict resolution is a strong underlying friendship: Fostering and deepening it is foundational to not only mitigating conflicts but also enhancing the overall quality and satisfaction of the relationship. We'll find out more about the importance of friendship in a romantic relationship in the next chapter.

WEEK 7: STRENGTHENING THE FRIENDSHIP BOND

 A successful relationship requires falling in love many times, always with the same person.

— MIGNON MCLAUGHLIN

When choosing your lifelong companion, you probably looked at them not only as your partner but also as a friend you could count on. You trusted and supported them, felt joyful, and respected them as they respected you. In fact, friendship is an important factor in a romantic relationship and must be cultivated over the years. If you let your daily responsibilities and duties define your routine, you might neglect your friendship, thus hindering trust and intimacy. That's why you must strengthen your bond to undertake your journey of mutual growth. In the next sections, you'll discover the significance of being friends with each other and how to nurture this relationship. Then, you'll find some useful activities to try together to learn to be good friends again.

WHY IT PAYS TO BE FRIENDS

If you've been friends with your lifelong companion for some time before becoming a couple, feel grateful because that's the most effective way of building a deep connection with them. Being friends before being partners has many advantages, as you learn things about each other that you probably wouldn't have if you immediately became a couple. If you weren't so lucky, there's nothing to worry about because you have the power to build a strong friendship right now.

Friendship is based on honesty, trust, and mutual respect, so you're more likely to share all your secrets and hidden thoughts and emotions with a friend rather than a brand-new partner, especially because you don't want to lose them as many people think. Therefore, a friendship allows you to be authentic and show your true self to others, thus making them understand who you are, what you want, and what you like. As you might guess, this situation puts you in a favorable position, as you immediately reveal yourself, and your partner knows all your qualities and flaws. Moreover, you build a deep level of appreciation and familiarity for each other's ideas, thoughts, interests, and values.

But what if you weren't so lucky to build a friendship before becoming a couple? Well, there's no problem at all! In fact, it doesn't matter if you become friends before or after becoming partners—friendship is always important and beneficial. Research has found that couples who share moments of intentional friendship are more likely to maintain vitality and connection in the long term and accept each other for who they are, thus reducing conflicts. When couples are friends, they appreciate each other's company more, respect each other, and are more likely to forgive each other after a mistake (Rimland, 2020). This doesn't mean that if you build friendship in your relationship, then you're 100% sure you'll solve all your problems and stay together for the rest of your life, but it surely helps.

Cultivating all types of connections requires effort and commitment, which is true both for your romantic relationship and your friendship: You might be able to nurture your intimate connection with your partner but neglect your friendship. For instance, you might remember to show kindness and appreciation to them by organizing a relaxing evening after a stressful day or not putting mayonnaise on their sandwich because they don't like it. However, you might neglect to stay updated about their daily life, so you might not know that in this period, they want to put mayonnaise in their sandwich or they feel worried about one of their friends facing a difficult moment.

The key to cultivating friendship in your romantic relationship is to know each other as no one else does. This means that you must accept change and acknowledge that they might grow as individuals and be different from who they were months or years ago. It's easy to believe that after we become 30 or 40 or after being in the same relationship for years, we stop changing, but that's not true. Therefore, it's important that you keep up-to-date with what your partner does every day and what happens in their personal life, at work, with their parents and relatives, and so on. If you want to be friends, you must make sure you know each other well and are emotionally close.

You might believe that being friends with your partner is not the most important thing for you right now and that you must focus on other aspects of your relationship. However, not cultivating your friendship can have negative consequences for you and your partner. You might feel a lack of commitment even if there's still physical attraction because you don't feel emotionally connected to each other, thus meaning that you have greater chances of experiencing a divorce or separation. You don't feel intimate with each other and can't find a goal that keeps you close and connected. Finally, you might feel like you're not in love anymore or your partner doesn't love you adequately because they appear not to know you well and appreciate you.

How can you understand if your relationship is based on friendship? First, you both genuinely like each other. If you weren't friends before becoming a couple, you might have focused on building a lasting relationship and how much you loved each other, thus forgetting to develop a solid friendship. Consequently, you didn't have time to know each other deeply and years later, you might find out you actually don't like each other because you're extremely different. After years of being together, liking each other is more important than loving each other, as it allows you to spend time together, enjoy doing things together, and appreciate every moment. If you and your partner are good friends, you enjoy spending every minute of your life together. You also feel comfortable talking about everything because you know you won't judge or criticize each other, and you will respect each other's opinions.

Moreover, being friends involves avoiding all drama and not seeing problems where there aren't any. If you have a solid friendship, you discuss everything honestly and don't feel like walking on eggshells all the time. In addition, you like trying new activities and involve each other in your hobbies and passions, thus creating a deep connection. But more importantly, you don't spend all day every day talking about what you have to do. Although duties are important, and we must all respect them, fun is also paramount, especially in long-lasting relationships. Therefore, you don't spend all the time planning what to do but dedicate a few minutes every day to just have fun and talk about nonsensical topics or things that make you laugh. To sum up, if you and your partner are good friends, then you're each other's favorite person in the world: You treat each other differently from anyone else, consider each other special, and will choose each other again and again over everyone else.

NURTURING FRIENDSHIP

If you realize you don't have a solid friendship with your partner, you might be curious to know ways in which you can cultivate this type of relationship. To start, you can follow some easy, practical tips that you can apply in your daily life.

- **Talk:** As mentioned many times, communication is paramount in all relationships, especially friendships. Take a few minutes every day to ask each other about your day, work, thoughts, emotions, and plans to cultivate a deep connection. If you notice you spend a lot of time on your smartphone or watching TV series, try to dedicate less time to such activities and more time to having chats. Remember that you can use various channels to communicate with each other, so if you don't have time to talk face-to-face, use your smartphone to call or send texts.
- **Spend more quality time together:** The key to nurturing a long-lasting friendship with your partner is spending more quality time together. Keep in mind that quality is more important than quantity, so you don't need to do things together all day, every day. Instead, you must enjoy every moment by paying your full

attention to each other. You don't have to always be
there for each other, as this would be impossible for
everyone. However, you must be fully present when
you're there, talk, and do things together. You must focus
on each other and avoid all distractions. When
considering how to spend quality time, think about what
you enjoy the most, even if it's not a long, deep
conversation or a serious activity—just have fun
together.

- **Show appreciation and affection:** Good friends
  show affection and appreciation to each other because
  they consider themselves the luckiest people in the world
  and value their profound connection, so that's what you
  must do with each other. Seize every opportunity to tell
  each other how grateful you are, thank each other for all
  the amazing things you do together, and express your
  love through hugs and kisses. You can also show
  appreciation and affection through texts and calls, so
  take a few minutes to text each other while working and
  send a friendly emoji or a few words like "I love you."

- **Celebrate milestones:** In the first few months or
  years of a relationship, you might have been used to
  celebrating important milestones, like your anniversary
  or birthday. Now, you probably spend less time
  celebrating the time passing by and consider milestones
  less exciting, like happens to many couples. However,
  dedicating time to celebrating cheerful events is essential
  to maintain a strong and positive connection. Therefore,
  do your best to plan activities and do something during
  special occasions. Remember that you don't need to
  organize the best day of the year, and you don't need to
  celebrate the same day—just take some time off work or
  plan a romantic evening at home after work.

- **Create new memories:** In Chapter 5, you learned how recalling good memories enhances intimacy and makes you closer to each other. However, having positive memories might not be enough to ensure a healthy relationship; you need to cultivate new ones, too. Maybe you were used to traveling a lot, trying new restaurants, cooking traditional meals from around the world, or sharing hobbies. Over the years, you might have abandoned your passions and focused on responsibilities and daily tasks. Now, it's time to bring them back to renovate your deep bond and build a meaningful relationship. If you want, you can think about activities that you were used to doing and that you would like to do again or try completely new experiences.

- **Be respectful:** One of the basic elements of healthy relationships is respect, which means feeling comfortable doing and saying everything because you don't criticize or judge each other but discuss things openly and honestly. The more respect you show, the deeper your connection will become, thus becoming good friends. Pay attention to the way you interact with each other every day and use more respectful language and tone of voice. When we're overwhelmed with duties, we might not consider the way we talk with our partners, thus ordering them to do things instead of asking or assuming they'll do something without talking about it with them. Such small gestures might look insignificant but might create conflicts and misunderstandings that accumulate over time, so try to avoid them as much as possible. Choose the right words and take more time to reflect on what you want to say before talking.

- **Support each other:** Another fundamental factor of healthy, long-lasting friendships is certainly support.

When your partner feels excited about something, don't dismiss their emotions. Instead, take the time to celebrate together and encourage them to do more, even if you don't feel good or aren't in the mood. The same is valid when they're going through tough times and need a shoulder to cry on or they don't believe in themself and their skills.

- **Take care of yourself:** This tip might look counterintuitive, as you should take care of your partner and not yourself. However, we can't take care of our loved ones if we don't value our mental and physical health first. Although we must be present for our significant others, support them, and celebrate during happy moments, we must also dedicate time to our overall well-being, which means doing things we enjoy, even if it involves spending time alone or with other people than our partners. Taking moments for our personal growth and checking in with our thoughts and emotions is paramount to building a healthy relationship where we know our value, what we want, and what we don't like. Only by knowing ourselves better and taking care of ourselves can we understand our partners and do what's best for them and us.

- **Laugh:** Last but not least, a good laugh is what distinguishes good friends from simple acquaintances. Watch comedy shows together, share funny stories, or look at funny videos on YouTube and Instagram. Take advantage of every occasion to laugh together, even in stressful and difficult moments, to enhance your mood and build a deeper connection.

WORKBOOK EXERCISES

Are you ready to strengthen the friendship bond even further in your daily life? Try the activities below!

Discovering Shared Hobbies

After being together for years, you might believe you've done everything, and there's nothing more you can try or that you'll never be able to achieve your dream goals after so long. Let go of despair and take the opportunity to try new activities you've always wanted to. During the seventh week, take some time to brainstorm ideas together and discuss things you would like to try. If you want, you can think about activities during the week and then share your ideas during the weekend. Use your imagination and include all the experiences you've always wanted to explore without hesitation. Then, discuss them, choose one that you both enjoy, and plan your actions. By facing the process of learning and discovery together, you create a bonding experience that makes you feel closer to each other, so don't miss this opportunity to deepen your connection.

Let's say you're both interested in mindfulness, as you've heard about it a lot and would like to give it a try. Find more information on the topic online and discuss ways in which you could practice it: Do you want to do everything by yourselves, or do you want to have some help, for example, by downloading an app with guided meditation exercises? Next, consider the best time to practice mindfulness for both and choose how much time you want to dedicate to it. After finding a compromise, try the activity and discuss it together: How does it make you feel? Do you want to keep practicing? Are you both comfortable with it and believe it could improve your mental and physical health? Make sure that you both enjoy the activity, and then just keep practicing!

If mindfulness is not for you and you want to try something different, you have plenty of opportunities, like participating in cooking classes, going hiking during the weekend, learning a new language, taking dance classes, volunteering, or traveling—even if it only involves exploring your neighborhood or city. Just think about your hobbies and passions and practice them together.

Walking Down Friendship Memory Lane

To practice this activity, you don't need to spend a lot of time, as a few minutes will be enough to share a significant memory. Take a leap into your past and think about a moment when you both felt a strong sense of friendship in your relationship. It can be a shared laugh over an inside joke, a tough time one of you faced while the other supported them, or a simple moment of companionship. After recalling a specific event, discuss what aspects of this memory made you feel connected to your partner as a good friend and consider ways in which you can cultivate more of these moments in your daily life.

Dream Team Activity Planning

As you discovered throughout the chapter, sharing hobbies and doing things together makes you feel closer and connected as friends. Therefore, you must do your best to plan as many activities as you can together. Identify a project or goal that requires teamwork, like organizing a community event, renovating a piece of furniture, or planning your next holiday. Then, outline all the steps you must take to plan and execute the chosen activity, focusing on the importance of working together. In fact, it's important that you're both equally involved and contribute in some way to achieving your goal. This way, you reinforce your connection and promote teamwork in your relationship. Finally, just complete the activity together!

In this chapter, you discovered the importance of friendship and how it enhances trust, support, and intimacy. However, the spirit of friendship and teamwork extends into all areas of a relationship—including managing finances. Financial harmony is another cornerstone of a strong partnership, where the hallmarks of a solid friendship—open communication, shared goals, and mutual support—are key to success. In the next chapter, you'll discover everything you need to tackle finances.

WEEK 8: TACKLING FINANCES

 Remember, the goal is resolve (or discuss) money issues in a way that creates harmony and not division.

— THE HEALTHY MARRIAGE

How comfortable do you feel talking about finances with each other? If you're not different from other couples, you probably struggle to discuss such a delicate topic and have always found it hard to be completely honest and open about the way you spend and save your money. If you don't have a joint account, you might keep a few secrets to yourself and don't reveal all the ways you spend your earnings. Even if you have one, you might be in charge of paying all the bills and keeping track of money while your partner is unaware of what happens in your bank account. Such situations are pretty common and might cause unwanted and unnecessary arguments. If you want to feel more connected to each other, you must start talking about money openly and honestly right now. In this chapter, you'll learn the negative effects of financial stress, what financial harmony is, how to achieve it, and useful strategies to talk about money effectively. Then, you'll find some practical activities you can try together in your daily life.

FINANCIAL HARMONY

One of the most common and recurrent topics couples argue about is money (Pace, 2020a). Managing finances is a delicate issue that might provoke negative effects in a relationship if not faced properly. If you're not open and honest with each other and struggle to talk about money effectively, you're more likely to experience stress, which hinders not only your mental and physical health but also your relationship. If you manage to discuss finances but never reach an agreement or a solution to your financial problems, you're also more likely to feel resentful toward each other. You might feel like your partner doesn't listen to or understand you and doesn't care about your thoughts, thus impairing communication. Interestingly, one study revealed that 68% of couples would feel more comfortable talking about their weight than the money they have in their savings account (Pace, 2020a). This is clear evidence that people struggle to talk about finances. However, avoiding such conversations might reduce trust and confidence in the relationship. Ultimately, poor money management can turn couples against each other and lead to divorce or separation.

How can you avoid such terrible consequences? You must find financial harmony, which involves developing a healthy relationship with money and being able to discuss it openly together. The keys to building financial harmony are shared goals, effective communication, budgeting, making decisions jointly, and financial resilience. You must work together to set and achieve your financial goals and make sure you both participate in the decision-making process, so you must both be aware of your financial situation and opportunities. Then, discuss money openly and honestly, without judging or blaming each other for your financial hurdles because they happen to anyone and can be solved only through collaboration. Next, create and stick to a budget that satisfies each other's needs and allows you to achieve your short-term and long-term financial goals without stress. By building financial harmony, you're more likely to face challenges effectively because you know how to manage risks as a couple, plan for unexpected events, and manage savings and emergency accounts. When dealing with money, working and thinking as a team is essential to achieving financial harmony and facing all economic obstacles.

STRATEGIES FOR EFFECTIVE FINANCIAL COMMUNICATION

The way you talk about money impacts your financial harmony and relationship, so how can you improve your conversations about finances? You can follow some easy tips!

- **Commit to regularly talking about money:** Consider finances as an ongoing conversation in your relationship, so never stop talking about it and get used to discussing how you plan to spend and save money regularly. For this reason, it's better to schedule a conversation about money in advance.
- **Talk to a financial planner:** If you realize you're not good at managing money on your own or you want to make sure you make the right economic decisions, speak to a financial planner. Thanks to them, you understand your current financial situation and how you can spend your money effectively.

- **Discuss how you plan to talk to your kids about money:** If you have children or plan to have them in the future, prepare to start talking about money when they're very little, like three or four years old. This way, you not only help them understand money management but also find a common goal to pursue and values to stick to.
- **Expect conflict:** As for every topic, you and your partner might have different ideas and it's okay. When you start discussing money healthily, don't expect to stop all disagreements but accept that they'll keep occurring from time to time—but you can face them with the right attitude.

If you want to make your conversations even deeper, here's a list of topics you might want to discuss with your partner.

- How are you going to manage your finances?
- How are you going to file taxes?
- How are you going to divide expenses?
- Discuss life insurance.
- Review health insurance plans.
- Check car insurance policies.
- Do you plan on having children?

WORKBOOK EXERCISES

After looking at some useful strategies to enhance your conversations about money, it's time to discover more exercises and practical activities to build financial harmony in your relationship.

Your Money Story

Your money story is a story about how money has influenced your relationship over the years and how it has impacted your daily choices as a couple. All relationships have a money story, and you might be aware of some of it but have never reflected on it as a whole. At the same time, you might know your personal relationship with money and how it influenced your life before being in the couple but not be aware of what your partner truly thinks about it. By knowing more about your and their money story, you identify the feelings and thoughts you associate with money and how having or not having it influences your mood and choices.

To practice this activity, start by taking some time for yourself and thinking about your relationship with money since you were a child: What did your parents think about it? What values did they pass down to you? How did you use it during adolescence and before being financially independent of your parents? How did you use it after having a stable job? How did you feel about spending and saving money? Go into as much detail as you can, and then think about how your relationship with money changed after becoming a partner. Finally, find a moment to discuss your thoughts deeply together.

Joint Financial Planning Session

Now, let's get more practical and look at your finances more in depth. To improve your relationship, you must be completely honest with each other and have a clear idea of your current and future financial situation. Therefore, conduct a comprehensive review of your finances, including every money you earn and spend, like your income, debts, savings, and investments. Keep in mind that you shouldn't judge your financial situation and blame each other for being in trouble or having little money. This should be a judgment-free, rational discussion.

Once you understand how you use your money right now, it's time to think about the future and plan your actions together. If you need help dividing the expenses and setting savings goals, look at the list below.

- **Marriage:** After analyzing your current situation, you must be honest about your pain points and acknowledge where you could do better. Common pain points include different spending habits, earning capacities, and ideas about managing bank accounts as a couple.
  Acknowledge that these difficulties are normal and work together to find effective solutions. Next, identify your individual and couple goals and discuss them together. Then, create an action plan where you consider opening a joint or savings account, prioritizing certain goals over others, setting deadlines to achieve your couple goals, and identifying all the little steps you must take. The more precise you are, the easier you'll achieve your objectives.
- **Relocation:** You might already have some experience with relocating, and you might worry about it because it didn't go well in the past, or you might plan to relocate in the future and wonder what the most essential steps are. Relocation is a complicated and long process that requires time, effort, and patience from both of you, so you must commit yourself to supporting each other and completing tasks together. You find a list of the basic steps to undertake before relocating below.
- **Budget:** Before relocating, you must know your current financial situation and be aware of how other people

could help you with the expenses, for example, if you move for work and your company provides financial help. Then, plan to save money regularly.

- **Research the costs:** While budgeting, dedicate some time to researching the costs of moving, which include transportation for you and your family to the new city, movers, renters or homeowners insurance, housing prices, real estate agencies, and so on.
- **Think about your furniture:** Sometimes, moving your furniture might be easy, and you might be so deeply attached to it that you want to keep it with you wherever you go. Other times, you might need to leave it behind due to costs or difficulties with transportation. Therefore, evaluate all your options and decide what's best to do together.
- **Research the area:** The area in which you will live is a fundamental factor in your future financial situation, so make sure to check nearby hospitals, parks, shopping malls, schools, and facilities to have an idea of what your monthly costs could be.
- **Deduct the expenses:** Finally, learn if you can deduct the expenses of traveling when doing your taxes, which is very likely if you move due to work.
- **Starting a new family:** If you plan to have a baby in the future, you might be worried about all your future expenses—and you're right! Raising a child is expensive and is very likely to revolutionize your current financial situation, so you must prepare for it. In general, you must consider not only short-term goals but also long-term ones, as you'll probably need a lot more money when your child grows up and goes to college. It might seem excessive to think about college even before your baby is born, but it's necessary to ensure you save

enough money. Here are some useful tips to start a new family.

- **Review your health insurance:** If you have health insurance, it can help you pay some of the costs of having a baby, so contact your insurer to know more about it.
- **Consider family leave:** Discover how much leave you're entitled to and if it's paid or not before having a baby, so you can organize together and have an idea of how much time you'll be able to spend with your newborn baby.
- **Think about childcare:** Consider if you want to hire a babysitter, place your baby in childcare, or take care of them on your own. Check out all your options and choose the one that better suits your needs based on your financial availability.
- **Set up a budget:** Think about all the money you would need to spend after your child is born. Make sure to include diapers, babysitter's fees, clothing, food, bedding, and so on. If you want, you can ask for help from other parents or friends who have children.
- **Save as much as you can:** Emergencies happen all the time, but they might occur more often with a baby, so top off your emergency savings and make sure to always have money saved.
- **Open an education savings account:** The further you think ahead, the easier you'll reach your goals without stress, so start thinking about your child's education now and save as much as you can. Keep in mind that you don't need to save hundreds of money every year, as you have time, but put some in your education savings account regularly.

- **Retirement:** Sooner or later, we'll all retire and need money to live a happy and peaceful life, so it's better to start thinking about it now. Before setting up any budget, have a deep conversation together to discuss your expectations about retirement: Where do you want to go? Do you want to stay close to relatives? What do you want to do during the day? Do you want to keep working in some way? By asking yourselves these questions, you have an idea of what you want to do when you retire and if your thoughts align. Next, choose the option that suits best both of you and start saving. As you probably won't retire in the near future, you have plenty of time to put money in your savings account; just make sure to do it regularly and not be tempted to use it for other expenses or emergencies.

Financial Boundaries

In Chapter 6, you learned about boundaries in general and discovered that financial ones involve how comfortable you feel talking about money with your partner. You also tried a useful activity to set healthy boundaries, but you can go more into detail and learn techniques to identify, establish, and express your financial boundaries. Follow the steps below.

1. **Define your limits:** If you've never thought about financial boundaries, it's time to do so. Think about your relationship with money, taking inspiration from the activity called "Your Money Story" you discovered above. Define what's inside and outside of your comfort zone, considering how you feel comfortable earning, spending, saving, and lending money. In addition, ask yourself if you're willing to open a joint account with

your partner or if you feel more comfortable keeping two different accounts.

2. **Get clear:** When defining your limits, try to be as clear and precise as possible. For example, if you feel comfortable lending money, explain to whom, how, and when so that your partner has an unequivocal idea of how you feel about it.

3. **Provide context:** When communicating your boundaries to your partner, provide as much context as you can. Therefore, don't restrict yourself to telling them how you feel comfortable spending and saving money but explain the reasons behind your behaviors. This way, they'll better understand your point of view and will be more likely to respect it.

4. **Prepare for pushback:** If you change the way you interact with your partner due to your new financial boundaries, they might react negatively. For instance, they might not accept the fact that you don't feel comfortable lending money and ask you to do it anyway. In such cases, be consistent and reinforce your boundaries.

Creating a Dream Fund

Another funny activity you can try together is to start a savings fund to a shared dream or goal, like traveling, starting a family, or buying a home. How can you create a dream fund? Use the following tips!

1. **Divide expenses:** Consider your current financial situation and the way you manage expenses. For example, is one of you always paying even if they earn less money, or is only one of you responsible for your

bank account while the other is unaware of everything? If you notice some inequality between you, change the way you divide expenses and manage money to include both in the decision-making process and make sure you both contribute fairly.

2. **Get a joint bank account:** If you feel comfortable with it, a joint bank account is the best way to save money, time, and effort, as you'll share all your earnings and expenses. This way, it's also easier to keep track of how you both spend, save, and earn.

3. **Improve your lifestyle:** Making small changes to your lifestyle might help you save more easily and rapidly for your dream fund. For instance, you might eat out less often, plan cheaper dates, or automate your savings.

4. **Budget together:** Keep track of your earnings, expenses, and savings and talk about your dream fund regularly. Establish a rule to save money and commit to following it. If you want, you can schedule regular check-ins to keep track of your progress and discuss unexpected expenses.

Now, you know what financial harmony is and how to talk about money openly and honestly, thus fostering a positive and strong connection with each other. In fact, financial harmony is a crucial component of a well-rounded and forward-looking relationship. In the next chapter, we'll dive deep into the topic of planning and discover ways to think about your future together.

WEEK 9: PLANNING FOR THE FUTURE TOGETHER

 The best love is the kind that awakens the soul and makes us reach for more, that plants a fire in our hearts and brings peace to our minds. And that's what you've given me. That's what I'd hoped to give you forever.

— NICHOLAS SPARKS

In the previous chapter, we started talking about shared goals and financial planning. In fact, discussing your future as a couple is a fundamental factor in fostering a deep and long-lasting connection and undertaking mutual growth together. In the next sections, you'll discover the importance of setting common goals, how to support each other's personal growth without hindering your connection, and practical strategies to cultivate a dynamic relationship that thrives over time. Then, you'll find useful exercises to practice setting shared and individual goals.

SHARING GOALS

As you've been together for some time, you might have set some shared goals, like going on holiday abroad or saving to buy a new car or house. But as daily responsibilities and duties increase and make you feel overwhelmed, you might have stopped setting goals together to focus on the present and reach the end of the month. There's nothing to be ashamed of, as it happens to all couples in a long-term relationship. However, setting shared goals is paramount to building a deep connection and growing together. Thanks to them, you not only show your commitment and how much you care for each other, but you also develop healthy habits and learn to count on each other. Studies show that support from your partner allows you to reach goals more easily, and setting and pursuing them benefits both you and your partner's mental and physical health (Field, 2023). This means that they have incredibly positive effects on your relationship.

Although setting shared goals is important, it's not enough to make sure you achieve the expected results. In fact, you must collaborate and reflect on the types of goals you want to achieve together: If you agree and feel excited about your journey together, you're more likely to obtain great results. If you don't agree or one of you isn't 100% sure of a particular goal, you're more likely to fail. Consequently, you must listen to each other and pay attention to each other's needs and wants to set a suitable goal for both. In this case, effective communication is essential to improve your relationship, so don't judge each other and be flexible and open to each other's points of view. When setting shared goals, you might feel extremely motivated and start with a positive attitude, but obstacles might arise. The two things you must always do are communicate and compromise. If you set a goal and realize that you don't manage to achieve it for some reason, clearly explain it to your partner and discuss ways to improve the situation. Alternatively, if you thought you both agreed on a goal but discover that one of you is dissatisfied, communicate openly and do your best to find a compromise that suits both of you.

Let's say you set a goal to dedicate more time to sexual intimacy and decide to have intercourse twice a week. In the beginning, you both seem satisfied and committed to pursuing your goal. After some time, one of you thinks that having intercourse twice a week isn't enough, so you should have it more often. They express their opinion honestly and make their partner understand their point of view while the other listens carefully with an open mind. After realizing your shared goal isn't shared anymore, you adapt it and find a solution that benefits both, like having inter-course four times a week instead of twice.

If you want to set shared goals, you must be on the same page both about your lifestyle and future. Therefore, you must identify the activities you both enjoy doing in your daily lives, like reading or keeping fit, and how you see yourselves in the next two, five, or even ten years. The more shared goals you set, the more you develop a sense of partnership and deep connection with each other, so make a list of all the things you want to do together. Some examples include having children (which might require time and many deep conversations), deciding exotic places to travel to, buying a home, improving your mental and physical health, or organizing date nights weekly or monthly. When setting shared goals, keep in mind that you must both contribute and express your opinion honestly, so take all the time you need to discuss different goals and find the ones that you share and would like to achieve together.

INDIVIDUAL GROWTH WITHIN THE RELATIONSHIP

After looking at shared goals, it's time to understand the significance of individual ones, even if you're in a long-term relationship. When we become partners, we all tend to let go of our personal aspirations and consider ourselves as half of the couple who must work toward reaching relationship goals. Obviously, we must all value doing things together, especially planning the future and setting short and long-term objectives. However, relationship goals aren't the only important ones. As already mentioned, taking care of ourselves and valuing our thoughts, emotions, interests, and needs is essential for a healthy and positive connection with our partners. That's why we must pursue individual goals just as much as relationship ones.

When thinking about individual goals, you might be skeptical and react negatively because you associate them with being selfish and neglecting your partner. Well, that's what most people tend to think, but that doesn't correspond to reality. Taking care of yourself and following your dreams doesn't make you selfish— it improves your life satisfaction and happiness, consequently enhancing your relationship with your partner. Research also confirms that there's a significant correlation between individual aspirations and relationship satisfaction: The more you pursue your personal goals, the more you feel satisfied with your partner (Eva, 2023).

How is it possible? By following your dreams, you maintain a sense of purpose in your life independently from your relationship, so you feel more self-confident, satisfied, and capable. In other words, you feel empowered to do what you want and like. As you boost your mood, you spread your joy in the relationships and people around you, especially your partner. However, pursuing your personal goals has many more benefits: It improves your self-awareness and allows you to understand your inner self better. You become aware of what you want and need and use your skills wisely to achieve your goals. Thanks to self-awareness, you know yourself better and understand what you want and need in a relationship, thus making your voice heard. At the same time, you're better at identifying and accepting your partner's needs, thus increasing their satisfaction within the couple, too.

As you can see, pursuing individual goals has incredible effects on you, your partner, and your relationship in general. But how can you grow while being in a long-term relationship? Follow the tips below!

- **Know yourself:** As already mentioned, being self-aware allows you to know yourself better, pursue the goals you really want to achieve, and understand your needs and wants. To enhance self-awareness, dedicate some time to activities you enjoy and improve your skills in your professional and personal life. Even if you share many interests and hobbies with your significant other, it's important that you do things by yourself, too, so make sure to find at least one activity you enjoy doing on your own.
- **Ask for feedback:** To practice self-improvement, you must look objectively at your strengths and weaknesses, so you must ask for feedback from people you trust. You might believe your partner can certainly provide useful feedback, but that's not always true, as their perception of your skills might be biased. Therefore, ask your friends and relatives how they perceive your strengths and weaknesses and how you can improve.
- **Prioritize your friendships:** A good way of maintaining your identity and making sure you pursue

your goals is taking care of your friendships. As you've been in a relationship for a long time, you might have lost touch with old, dear friends. It's time to contact them and rebuild your connection. Even if your partner can challenge and motivate you, they can't offer you all the support and encouragement you require. After all, they can't fulfill all your needs alone—you also need other people in your life. Therefore, dedicate some time to your friendships, prioritizing the ones that make you feel better and support you.

- **Invest in people:** In general, interacting with different people not only helps you know yourself better but also changes your perspective on your relationship and helps you understand your partner's needs more deeply. Therefore, building connections with different people can improve your relationship in various ways. If you have the opportunity to meet someone new at work or get in touch with someone who might enrich your life, seize it.

- **Find a mentor:** When focusing on self-improvement and personal goals, you might make mistakes that could cost you your relationship, as happens to all of us. If you don't pay attention to your choices, you might end up hindering your connection with your lifelong companion. For this reason, it's important that you find a mentor or a person who's equally invested in your self-improvement journey and provides guidance. They should be someone who you trust and who cares a lot about you. This way, you know they'll always provide advice based on what's best for you and your relationship.

STRATEGIES FOR GROWING AS A COUPLE

After understanding the importance of individual goals and learning useful tips to pursue them while being in a relationship, it's time to focus on shared goals and ways to grow as a couple. Here, you will find a list of actionable advice on how you can foster mutual growth and pursue your objectives together.

- **Don't settle:** If you feel like you've settled, it's time to take action and do something to improve your relationship. Pay attention to your feelings and make sure you always know there's something more you can try together.
- **Accept conflict:** As you learned in Chapter 6, happy and satisfied couples aren't the ones who never argue but the ones who argue effectively. So, don't be afraid of conflict, but face it with the right attitude because it helps you improve your relationship.
- **Apologize:** Learn to say you're sorry unconditionally, without expecting anything in return. Take responsibility for your actions and make sure that your apology comes from your heart so that your partner knows you sincerely care about them and want to make things right when something bad happens.
- **Schedule time to discuss your relationship:** Throughout the book, you learned the significance of communicating and dedicating quality time to each other. In fact, scheduling regular conversations to discuss how you feel, what you need, and what you plan to do in the future is paramount. Taking a few minutes every few weeks to have a deep conversation about your relationship allows you to keep track of your emotions,

notice if something is wrong before it becomes too difficult to handle, and become aware of where you are.

- **Remember why you love each other:** After being together for so many years, you might easily forget why you love each other and why you decided to get together in the first place. As you already learned, fond memories play a crucial role in your relationship, so you must cultivate them. Whenever you feel upset about something your partner did or said, take a few seconds to recall a fond memory and ask yourself why you love them. If you want, you can even write down a list of 10 reasons and keep it close. This way, your negative emotions will reduce and you'll focus on more positive ones.

- **Make space for each other:** To develop a strong relationship, you must be conscious of your space. You mustn't suffocate each other and do things together all the time but balance your needs and responsibilities. Understand that work and other relationships are important, too, and cultivate them by yourself. Make sure that you both agree to make space for each other and accept it.

- **Work as a team:** Happy and satisfied couples are friends who work together toward the same goals. They're like a team who collaborate to improve and become better people, and that's exactly what you should aim for in your relationship. Even when arguments arise, don't see each other as an enemy to defeat but as team members who pursue the same goal. This way, you'll tackle conflicts and disagreements more effectively.

WORKBOOK EXERCISES

Are you ready to practice some tailored exercises that will help you combine individual growth with shared goals? Try the following activities!

Growth Goals

To set growth goals as a couple, you must work on yourselves first, so you must think about your individual goals. Take some time throughout this ninth week to consider all the goals you want to achieve in the future, focusing on the aspirations that might improve your relationship in one way or another. For example, you might set a goal to go walking for 20 minutes every day after work to increase your physical health and fight stress. On one hand, you might consider your actions selfish and dismiss them as ways to hinder your relationship. On the other hand, consider that your mental and physical health is paramount, and if you don't take care of yourself, you struggle to care for your partner, too. The more relaxed you feel, the more calmly and peacefully you'll interact with them. When thinking about how your individual goals can improve your relationship, take all the time you need—I'm sure you'll find good answers to your questions. At the end of the week, get together and discuss your personal goals, keeping in mind that they are opportunities to deepen your connection and enhance the overall health of your relationship. Therefore, avoid judging each other or jumping to conclusions.

Learning a New Skill

Doing things together allows you to develop a deeper connection with each other, but you also need to practice activities on your own. Therefore, commit to learning a new skill that you don't share with each other to grow as individuals. Remember to set a specific goal that allows you to keep track of your progress, understand when you achieve important objectives, and believe in yourself. The way you perceive your opportunities and skills greatly influences your success: If you don't believe in yourself, you're more likely to fail. Then, use all the available tools to make the learning process easier and funnier. For instance, watch YouTube videos and try things firsthand to have a clear idea of how to do them. If you want, you can also ask for help from someone who has already mastered the skill you want to practice and make them your mentor or coach. Finally, to make sure you learn something new, do it again and again. Don't let yourself down if you make mistakes or have tough times because they're part of the learning process. Instead, keep practicing and do your best to achieve your goals.

If you don't know where to start, here's a list of funny and enriching activities you can try on your own.

- Study a foreign language.
- Practice photography.
- Use Photoshop.
- Try gardening.
- Draw.
- Learn basic home and car repairs.
- Declutter your home.
- Cook.
- Play an instrument.
- Read more.

In this chapter, you learned the importance of setting shared goals and supporting individual growth to maintain a positive and healthy relationship over time. In fact, planning for the future together is a profound act of love and commitment. While undertaking your journey toward mutual growth, you'll reach important milestones that will improve your relationship and that you mustn't undervalue. All achievements, even the smallest ones, are worth celebrating because they build a deep connection between you and your partner. In the final chapter, you'll take a moment to reflect on your journey thus far and honor the dedication and shared visions that have been cultivated, thus celebrating love and commitment.

WEEK 10: CELEBRATING LOVE AND COMMITMENT

 Real love has little to do with falling. It's a climb up the rocky face of a mountain, hard work, and most people are too selfish or too scared to bother. Very few reach the critical point in their relationship that summons the attention of the light and the dark, that place where they will make a commitment to love no matter what obstacles—or temptations—appear in their path.

— STACEY JAY

You've finally reached the culminating chapter and last week of your journey toward mutual growth. To be successful and improve your relationship, acknowledge both individual and mutual progress, thus valuing each other's contributions during the journey and appreciating all the steps you've taken until now. Celebrating your love and commitment toward each other is essential to have a strong, deep, and long-lasting relationship. In the next sections, you'll discover alternative and creative ways of expressing love in your daily lives and tips to uphold commitment. Then, you'll look at some useful exercises to celebrate love and commitment.

EXPLORING VARIED EXPRESSIONS OF LOVE

Throughout the book, you have discovered traditional ways to express love to each other, focusing on your love language and your preferred ways to receive and give affection. However, there are plenty of ways in which you can show love and appreciation to each other. We all tend to believe that love is a natural feeling that we experience or not, but we actually have more say in it than we're used to believing. Research has found that taking more loving actions makes couples feel more in love with each other (Firestone, 2022). This means that the more effort you put into showing love to your partner, the more they'll feel loved and feel love toward you. Even after being together for years, little or big expressions of love have the power to improve your relationship and avoid stagnation.

Instinctively, we tend to express love the way we would like our partners to do: If we enjoy physical touch, we think the best way to show our love is by hugging and kissing them all the time. However, this might not be their preferred way of receiving love, as you also learned in Chapter 2. Instead of focusing on what you like and want from your partner, think about their perspective and what they would like from you. Put yourself in their shoes and express love in a way they appreciate. If you're not sure about their preferences, just pay attention to their actions: If they show your love to you by writing romantic texts or listening to you carefully, these are probably the things they would appreciate the most from you. The most important thing to keep in mind is never to believe that you instinctively know what your partner wants and needs.

Let's consider an example. Imagine you and your partner arguing every time you celebrate your anniversary. One of you puts a lot of effort into organizing something special while the other one doesn't seem to care. The first one feels rejected and not appreciated, while the second feels pressured, so you both are disappointed by the celebration of your anniversary. Why does this happen? That's because you don't put yourselves in each other's shoes. One likes expressing love by making big, romantic plans to celebrate important occasions, while the other believes that huge events mean nothing without small, thoughtful gestures made every day. After taking each other's perspective, you can re-evaluate your anniversary and see it from a different light. You consider each other's point of view, and the one who likes organizing big events understands and accepts that their partner gives more value to other forms of expression of love while the latter puts more effort into celebrating the anniversary. This way, you increase relationship satisfaction and happiness.

But what if you struggle to understand each other's preferred ways to express and receive love? Well, communication is paramount, as always. In addition to looking at each other's body language and paying attention to the things you both like doing to express your love toward each other, talk about different expressions of love and what you prefer. Listen to each other carefully and check in with each other to understand if you clearly interpret each other's words. Keep in mind that no one of us is good at mind-reading, so it's better to ask than presume.

Here, you will find a list of examples of alternative and creative ways of expressing love toward each other.

- **Be their cheerleader:** No matter if your partner makes a mistake or achieves a small, positive result— you're there to support them at all times. If they have a dream and are afraid of making it real, you encourage them to use all their skills, stay positive, and never give up. If they feel down because they failed at something, you cheer them up and emphasize what they can learn from their failures and how they can do better next time.

- **Acknowledge their efforts:** In Chapter 3, you discovered the importance of feeling grateful toward your partner. Well, you can put that information into practice by appreciating all the efforts they've made on undertaking this journey and working with you to improve the relationship. Acknowledge their commitment to follow this workbook and become a better partner, like you're doing.

- **Love unconditionally:** Many romantic movies talk about unconditional love like it's something you can achieve easily. However, the true meaning of "unconditional" is often overlooked. To love your partner unconditionally, you must learn to appreciate them for who they are without expecting anything in return. You don't stay with them because they're nice to you and always shower you with love, appreciation, and affection but because you genuinely like them. You relish every laugh you share, enjoy spending time with them and doing things together, appreciate all their qualities, and acknowledge all their flaws and shortcomings without judging them.

- **Replace "I love you" with "What I love about you:"** This is another alternative way of expressing your love. Saying "I love you" helps your partner understand your emotions but doesn't let them know why. By listing the things you love about them, you make them feel more appreciated.

- **Make them feel like they're the only person in the world when you're surrounded by people:** How can you do it? It seems a hard task but it's pretty simple: Just make eye contact every once in a while. When you're surrounded by people, you might be distant and talk with others, so you're not focused on your partner. However, you can show them you always think about them by looking at them every now and then.

- **Surprise them:** A surprise every now and then is necessary to express love and affection! You can do whatever you want, so use your imagination. For instance, replace an evening watching Netflix with a walk around your neighborhood, do something you know they like, or ask them what their perfect day looks like and make it happen in one way or another. You have plenty of opportunities to surprise your partner with small gestures every day or bigger plans.

- **Help them stay healthy:** Another simple thing you can do for your partner is help them stay healthy. If they want to make their habits healthier and eat less junk food or go walking more often, encourage and support them. Help them stay motivated and keep track of their progress to allow them to achieve their goals.

CHOOSING TO COMMIT

In addition to expressing love, showing commitment is also paramount to developing a healthy and strong connection with each other. In the past, you've probably shown your commitment in various ways, as you wanted to display your love, affection, and interest in the relationship. As the years go by, your commitment might have decreased due to daily responsibilities, stress, financial problems, children, and many other reasons. In any case, a lack of commitment in a long-term relationship might surface and cause various problems for the couple. For example, they might feel disconnected from each other, thus drifting apart and even cheating on each other because they fall into temptation more easily and rapidly or simply stop trusting each other. As you can see, a lack of commitment might lead to serious problems in a long-term relationship, but the most crucial one is that couples don't spend time and effort repairing possible damages. If you don't feel committed to each other, you struggle to see the path forward and find reasons why you should put effort into improving yourself within the relationship. That's why commitment is essential, and a lack of it might lead to the end of a marriage or long-term connection.

In fact, when you're committed to each other and your relationship, you're convinced to stay together and agree to unwritten rules like loving and taking care of each other. Thanks to commitment, you feel safe and secure and know you can count on each other in both good and bad times. By enhancing it, you foster intimacy, support, mutual growth, trust, and long-term fulfillment, thus improving your connection, feeling closer to each other, and being willing to repair any damage that has impacted your relationship over the years. However, keep in mind that increasing commitment requires effort on both parts and must be a choice—not a forcing. To undertake the journey of mutual growth together, you must both be committed and do your best to improve. If only one of you puts effort into it, the journey won't lead to a deeper and stronger connection. At the same time, you can't force your partner to increase their commitment to the relationship if that's not what they want because it must come from within them and must be cultivated and strengthened over time. If you notice you're not as committed as before in the relationship and you're not willing to improve, think about your priorities and if underlying issues affect your commitment.

It's normal to feel a bit less committed to each other after years of being together, but it doesn't mean you must abandon all hope! If you focus on all the things you love about each other and your relationship, you can overcome this obstacle and achieve a deeper connection. Remember that hard times pass like good ones, so even if you're having a difficult moment, it doesn't mean that it will last forever. If you both commit to improving, you have the power to repair your relationship and grow together. In some cases, ending things might seem like the best and easiest option, but you shouldn't consider it lightly for various reasons. First, thinking about how someone else might fulfill you more than your current partner might seem an exciting and comfortable thought right now, but it's not true. In most cases, you'll feel happier for a short period and then have other or even the same problems. If you chose to be in a long-term relationship with your significant other and have come this far, it must mean something: They're right for you; you just need to adjust and improve together. Don't expect things to be easier or find fulfillment by breaking up. Last but not least, keep in mind that working together through hard times seems difficult but pays back because you'll become stronger as a couple.

Are you ready to increase your commitment and make sure to uphold it at all times? Follow the tips below.

- **Create a commitment statement:** Write down a statement where you show your commitment to each other, emphasizing the purpose and goals of your relationship and the boundaries that make you feel safe and secure.

- **Don't change your partner:** After being together for some time, you might try to change each other, even without realizing it. However, to uphold your commitment, show each other the effort you put into improving yourself—not your partner.
- **Greet each other every day:** Greet each other after waking up in the morning, before going to work, and before turning the lights off at night. Seize any opportunity to wish each other a good day to lift your mood.
- **Discuss your dreams and goals:** To stay on the same page, dedicate time to discuss your dreams and goals freely. When you talk about the future together, you know you can count on each other in the long term, thus increasing your commitment.
- **Compromise:** Show each other that you're willing to consider your relationship above everything else, even your personal needs and wants, by compromising. Once one partner compromises, the other is more likely to do the same and they increase their chances of pursuing shared goals.
- **Create and practice family traditions:** Put effort into developing family traditions and practice them regularly. For instance, create movie nights, date nights, special holidays, and so on. By creating family traditions, you develop a deep connection with each other and make sure to always have fun together.

WORKBOOK EXERCISES

In the last week of your journey toward mutual growth, commit to practicing the following three activities to uphold commitment and celebrate love!

Planning a Renewal of Vows Ceremony

If you've been married for a long time, it's time to renew your vows to celebrate how you've grown and improved together and express your love and commitment once again. I'm sure the vows you'll think about this time are different from the ones you came up with when you first married, but that's normal and a good sign that things have changed, but you're still together. In fact, when writing your vows, keep in mind that they should reflect your journey, values, and future aspirations, so they shouldn't be the same as the first time. In addition, you must make them as personal as possible so that they clearly represent the growth and deeper understanding developed through this journey. When planning your renewal of vows ceremony, make it intimate and pleasant. If you've organized a big marriage the first time, it doesn't mean you have to do it again. If you prefer a private event with just a few best friends and the closest relatives, that's fine.

Exchange of Love Letters

This activity is as simple as it seems: You must exchange love letters at the end of this week. Take a few minutes or half an hour during the week to think about what to write in your letters and then schedule a day and time to exchange them. Make sure to emphasize honesty and vulnerability and express love, gratitude, and commitment. You don't have to write an intricate poem, use complicated language, or write 10 pages of letter—just go with the flow and see what comes out. If you make mistakes or aren't satisfied with your writing, there's nothing to worry about, as the important thing is the clarity of your words and message.

After exchanging letters, you can decide to cultivate this activity and repeat it every year if you both enjoy it. Just think about a day when you want to exchange your letters yearly, like your anniversary, and commit to getting together. This way, you have one year to think about your letters and write them. Make sure to hide them properly so that you don't find and read them before the planned day! If you need some hints on what to include, write down funny or romantic anecdotes to show how you love your partner or talk about your dreams for your future together.

Hosting a Celebration of Love Event

If you're not married, you might not have the opportunity to renew your vows, but this doesn't mean that you can't celebrate your love and commitment! Even if you're married, you can try this activity: Hosting a celebration of love event. Instead of planning a renewal of vows, simply plan a day or two to celebrate your love and commitment however you prefer. You don't have to do anything particular or invite others—just celebrate in your favorite way. For instance, you can plan a gathering with friends and relatives where you all eat together and have fun while you tell stories about how your relationship improved recently. Alternatively, plan a romantic weekend getaway, ensuring you get all the details right and book in advance. Other examples of a celebration of love event involve organizing a picnic under the stars in the middle of nature or planning an adventure in the wild, like hiking, rock climbing, or taking a hot air balloon ride. If you use your imagination and creativity, I'm sure you'll come up with ideas you both enjoy and are thrilled to try together!

This last chapter emphasized the importance of celebrating love and commitment to build a strong and deep connection. Every day offers a new opportunity to celebrate love and commitment: Keep exploring, growing, and expressing your love toward each other in ways that deepen your connection.

CONCLUSION

This 10-week journey of mutual growth has finally come to an end and has taught you a lot about your past, your current situation, and what you can do in the future. Thanks to it, you see your relationship and lifelong companion in a renewed light and are ready to continue your journey together as a stronger and happier couple.

During the first week, you took a step back and looked at your past to understand what's going on right now and discovered how the attachment you developed during your childhood is influencing your current interactions with your partner. In the second week, you learned the significance of effective communication and how to put it into practice by building active listening and assertiveness skills and paying attention to nonverbal cues. You also discovered the five languages of love and how to use them to understand how both you and your partner like receiving and giving love to each other.

The third week taught you the importance of appreciation and showed you ways in which you can be thankful for your partner

and what they do for you. Remember that you can show gratitude in your daily life by making small gestures that lift their
mood and make them feel loved and appreciated. The fourth
week focused on trust and showed you how important it is for the
development of a strong and deep connection. If trust is broken
in your relationship, you can repair it by maintaining your
promises, telling the truth, and being honest.

During the fifth week, you discovered the different types of intimacy and how to use all of them to feel more comfortable with
each other. Keep in mind that intimacy goes well beyond physical
touch, and you must both feel secure and safe in the relationship.
During the sixth week, you learned that conflict is an essential
element, and you can't avoid it. In fact, the healthiest and
strongest couples aren't the ones who never argue but the ones
who solve conflicts constructively. Therefore, you must put effort
into listening to each other carefully, valuing each other's point of
view, and finding a solution that benefits both.

In the seventh week, you uncovered ways to become good friends
and value friendship in your relationship, as being friends is just
as important as being partners. You must count on each other,
have fun, and talk about everything without fear of being judged,
criticized, or rejected. The eighth week focused on a more practical problem many couples must face: finances. Among all the
boundaries, financial ones help you set limits in which you feel
comfortable earning, spending, and saving your money. The
more precise you are in setting them, the more your partner will
respect them. In addition, you must discuss finances regularly to
plan your future together and build financial harmony.

In the ninth week, you analyzed your future together more in-
depth and learned ways to plan your next moves. In particular,
you discovered how to set shared and individual goals for the

well-being of your relationship. By taking the time to dedicate to your dreams and aspirations, you enrich your connection and put more effort into pursuing relationship goals. Finally, the last week taught you ways to enhance love and commitment to deepen your bond and trust each other for the rest of your life.

After all, the key element to continuing this journey of mutual growth together and improving your relationship is to learn to love each other unconditionally. Show gratitude without expecting anything in return, and appreciate each other for who you are and what you like, not only for all the things you do for each other. Have fun making plans together, not because you have to but because you enjoy spending time with each other and thinking about your future together. Respect each other's point of view, even when you don't agree, and see conflicts as opportunities to learn rather than obstacles. The more you show unconditional love toward each other, the more you grow as a couple and deepen your connection.

At this point, you have all the tools you need to continue your journey of mutual growth together. Consider this book as a starting point and guiding light that illuminates your path whenever you need it. If you notice you can use a refresh or enjoyed undertaking this journey once, you can do it again after some time. Moreover, don't limit yourself to practicing the suggested activities for each week once and forget about them, but integrate them into your daily life to ensure you keep putting effort into your relationship. Let this journey you've taken together be a living testament to the enduring power of love and commitment. May you continue to grow, love, and celebrate each other every day.

REFERENCES

Adrian. (2020, May 28). *Commitment quotes: The very best.* Happily Committed. https://happilycommitted.com/commitment-quotes/

Babauta, L. (2021, February 20). *Positive feedback loops.* Zen Habits. https://zenhabits.net/positive-feedback/

Bedosky, L. (2024, February 5). *What are the 5 love languages (and how can you practice yours)?* EverydayHealth. https://www.everydayhealth.com/emotional-health/what-are-love-languages/

Bergeron, K. (2016, June 2). *How to financially plan for relocating.* Quicken. https://www.quicken.com/blog/how-financially-plan-relocating/

Better Health Channel. (2021). *Relationships - creating intimacy.* Better Health Channel. https://www.betterhealth.vic.gov.au/health/HealthyLiving/relationships-creating-intimacy

Bickham, S. (2023, September 4). *10 types of intimacy in a relationship.* https://www.choosingtherapy.com/types-of-intimacy/

Byrne, C. (2023, April 5). *7 tips for talking about money with your partner (and other important people in your life).* Everyday Health. https://www.everydayhealth.com/emotional-health/tips-for-talking-about-money-with-your-partner/

Cherry, K. (2022, May 26). *4 types of attachment styles.* Verywell Mind. https://www.verywellmind.com/attachment-styles-2795344

Cherry, K. (2023, February 22). *What is attachment theory?* Verywell Mind. https://www.verywellmind.com/what-is-attachment-theory-2795337#toc-history-of-the-attachment-theory

Chowdhury, M. R. (2019, April 9). *The neuroscience of gratitude and effects on the brain.* PositivePsychology.com. https://positivepsychology.com/neuroscience-of-gratitude/

Christian, K. (2023, April 25). *How to grow alongside your partner—even when you've both changed.* The Good Trade. https://www.thegoodtrade.com/features/how-to-stay-together/

Cicero, M. T. (n.d.). *A quote by Marcus Tullius Cicero.* GoodReads. https://www.goodreads.com/quotes/72368-gratitude-is-not-only-the-greatest-of-virtues-but-the

Coambs, E. (2022, January 6). *How knowing your money story improves your relationship.* Healthy Love and Money. https://www.healthyloveandmoney.com/blog/how-knowing-your-money-story-improves-your-relationship

Cobb, N. (n.d.). *Fair fighting rules for couples.* Cobb & Associates, Inc. https://www.nathancobb.com/fair-fighting-rules.html

Constructive conflict vs destructive conflict: Managing conflict effectively. (2020, November 25). Aristotle's Cafe. https://www.aristotlescafe.com/blog/constructive-conflict/

Covey, S. R. (2019). *Stephen R. Covey quotes.* GoodReads. https://www.goodreads.com/author/quotes/1538.Stephen_R_Covey

Cuncic, A. (2024, February 12). *7 active listening techniques for better communication.* Verywell Mind. https://www.verywellmind.com/what-is-active-listening-3024343

Curtis, T. (2023, January 10). *6 ways to set financial boundaries.* NerdWallet. https://www.nerdwallet.com/article/finance/setting-boundaries

Cusido, C. (2014, May 17). *How to nourish different types of intimacy in your relationship.* Psych Central. https://psychcentral.com/relationships/nourishing-the-different-types-of-intimacy-in-your-relationship#spiritual-intimacy

Deras, C. (2022, June 29). *Top 10 financial topics to discuss with your partner.* LinkedIn. https://www.linkedin.com/pulse/top-10-financial-topics-discuss-your-partner-/

Discover your attachment style. (2020). Attachment Project. https://www.attachmentproject.com/attachment-style-quiz/

Embrace new life. (n.d.). Life, Love, Marriage - Counseling & Consulting. https://embracenewlife.com/wp-content/uploads/2020/11/ENL-Couples-Worksheets.pdf

Eva. (2023, May 25). *Personal growth in a relationship: Can it help your marriage?* Connect Again. https://connect-again.com/post/personal-growth-in-a-relationship

Evans, L. N. (2017, July 14). *15 reasons why you must build a friendship before a relationship.* Marriage.com. https://www.marriage.com/advice/relationship/friendship-before-relationship-12-reasons-why-you-should-accept-being-his-friend/

Fen Chan, S. (2023, September 21). *How to create an emotionally safe space in your marriage.* Focus on the Family. https://www.family.org.sg/articles/how-to-create-an-emotionally-safe-space-in-your-marriage/

Field, B. (2023, June 26). *How to set relationship goals with your partner.* Verywell Mind. https://www.verywellmind.com/how-to-set-relationship-goals-with-your-partner-7547010

Finley, S. (2024, January 17). *8 powerful trust exercises for couples.* Paired Magazine. https://www.paired.com/articles/trust-exercises-for-couples

Firestone, L. (2022, August 27). *How to love your partner the way they want to be loved.* Psychology Today. https://www.psychologytoday.com/intl/blog/compassion-matters/202208/how-love-your-partner-the-way-they-want-be-loved

Fisher, M. (2015, September 21). *How to increase physical intimacy in a relationship: 15 tips.* Marriage.com. https://www.marriage.com/advice/physical-intimacy/4-essential-tips-to-improve-physical-intimacy-in-a-marriage/

5 ways to build trust in a relationship. (2023, July 25). UK Therapy Guide. https://uktherapyguide.com/5-ways-to-build-trust-in-a-relationship

Flinn, A. (2020, May 13). *I'm a couples therapist, and these are the 6 biggest communication issues I see in relationships.* Well+Good. https://www.wellandgood.com/communication-issues-in-relationships/

Forrest, S. (2022, November 14). *Study shows the power of "thank you" for couples.* University of Illinois Urbana-Champaign. https://news.illinois.edu/view/6367/772090023

Glass, L. J. (2019, January 22). *The importance of trust in a relationship.* Pivot. https://www.lovetopivot.com/the-importance-of-trust-in-a-relationship/

Green, S. (2016, January 28). *11 tips that help couples keep growing in a relationship.* LifeHack. https://www.lifehack.org/358731/11-tips-that-help-couples-keep-growing-relationship

Growth in relationships: 5 ways to create a growth-oriented relationship. (2023, August 14). Anchor Light Therapy Collective. https://anchorlighttherapy.com/how-to-have-a-growth-oriented-relationship/

Gupta, S. (2021a, September 12). *What's the difference between hearing and listening?* Verywell Mind. https://www.verywellmind.com/hearing-vs-listening-what-s-the-difference-5196734

Gupta, S. (2021b, December 27). *Why trust matters in your relationship and how to build it.* Verywell Mind. https://www.verywellmind.com/how-to-build-trust-in-a-relationship-5207611

Harris, R. (2023, March 30). *A breach of trust.* LinkedIn. https://www.linkedin.com/pulse/breach-trust-richard-harris-ph-d/

The Healthy Marriage. (2020, August 4). *5 tips to help you get your marriage and money problems in order.* The Healthy Marriage. https://thehealthymarriage.org/marriage-and-money-problems/

Helen. (2019, December 2). *The love letter ceremony.* Treasured Ceremonies. https://treasuredceremonies.co.uk/a-love-letter-ceremony-is-a-ceremony-within-a-ceremony-in-which-letters-are-written-and-locked-away-for-safe-keeping/

How to grow individually in a relationship? 6 pro tips. (2022, April 19). Marriage.com. https://www.marriage.com/advice/relationship/grow-individually-in-a-relationship/

The importance of commitment in a relationship. (2023, March 13). Best Self Forward. https://bestselfforwardtherapy.com/the-importance-of-commitment-in-a-relationship/

The importance of communication in relationships. (2021, June 23). Marriage.com. https://www.marriage.com/advice/communication/importance-of-communication-in-relationships/

Intimacy and relationships. (2018). Options for Sexual Health. https://www.optionsforsexualhealth.org/facts/sex/intimacy-and-relationships/

Ioannou, M. (2022, March 21). *100 goals for marriage to strengthen your relationship.* GenTwenty. https://gentwenty.com/goals-for-marriage/

Jones, B. (2023, April 5). *5 types of intimacy and how to build it in a relationship.* Verywell Health. https://www.verywellhealth.com/intimacy-7253066

Jones, R. (2022, December 5). *77 relationship goals quotes to inspire couples in 2024.* Happier Human. https://www.happierhuman.com/relationship-goals-quotes/

Kamuntu, B. (2022, January 5). *Openness is an important aspect of relationships.* Monitor. https://www.monitor.co.ug/uganda/lifestyle/heart-to-heart/openness-is-an-important-aspect-of-relationships-3673230

Lau, J. (2023, April 25). *7 strategies for learning new skills.* Zapier. https://zapier.com/blog/learning-new-skills/

The love language quiz. (2023). Love Languages. https://5lovelanguages.com/quizzes/love-language

Making moments: Creative ways to celebrate anniversaries. (2023, June 10). LinkedIn. https://www.linkedin.com/pulse/making-moments-creative-ways-celebrate-anniversaries-event-needz/

Married Fun. (n.d.). *How to handle a lack of commitment within your marriage.* Married Fun. https://marriedfun.org/content/how-to-handle-a-lack-of-commitment-within-your-marriage

McLaughlin, M. (n.d.). *Mignon McLaughlin quote.* BrainyQuote. https://www.brainyquote.com/quotes/mignon_mclaughlin_106607

Muenter, O. (2022, June 12). *12 fun hobbies for couples to enjoy together.* Brides. https://www.brides.com/fun-hobbies-for-couples-5115724

Ncube, C. (2023, April 20). *The emotional & personal bank account.* LinkedIn. https://www.linkedin.com/pulse/emotional-personal-bank-account-cheraine-ncube/

Newsome, T. (2016, June 1). *11 little things you're doing to sabotage trust.* Bustle. https://www.bustle.com/articles/163407-11-little-things-youre-doing-that-can-sabotage-trust-in-your-relationship

Nicole, A. (2019, August 22). *3 kind, simple & effective ways to communicate your boundaries.* Medium. https://headway.ginger.io/3-kind-simple-effective-ways-to-communicate-your-boundaries-46dad0989e79

116 deep questions that will strengthen your connection. (2023, October 27). Personal Creations Blog. https://www.personalcreations.com/blog/deep-questions

Pace, R. (2020a, September 2). *5 ways financial problems negatively affect your marriage, and tips on how to solve them together.* AllBusiness. https://www.allbusiness.com/5-ways-financial-problems-negatively-affect-your-marriage-and-tips-on-how-to-solve-them-together-129531-1.html

Pace, R. (2020b, November 10). *Can marriage survive without friendship?* Marriage.com. https://www.marriage.com/advice/relationship/can-marriage-survive-without-friendship/

Perry, E. (2022, April 13). *How building healthy boundaries is the key to work relationships.*

BetterUp. https://www.betterup.com/blog/healthy-boundaries-in-relation ships

Practicing gratitude as a couple. (n.d.). Intelligent Change. https://www.intelli gentchange.com/blogs/read/practicing-gratitude-as-a-couple

Rabinowitz, L. (2021, May 10). *15 questions to ask your significant other to deepen your trust & confidence in each other.* Counselor for Couples. https://counselorforcou ples.com/15-questions-to-ask-your-significant-other-to-deepen-your-trust-confidence-in-each-other/

Raypole, C. (2020, August 20). *Assertive communication is healthy, not "bossy" — here's why.* Healthline. https://www.healthline.com/health/assertive-communica tion

Reid, S. (2024, February 5). *Gratitude: The benefits and how to practice it.* Help-Guide.org. https://www.helpguide.org/articles/mental-health/gratitude.htm

Rimland, A. (2020, February 6). *Friendship: The most important ingredient in a relation-ship.* Thrive Couple & Family Counseling Services. https://thrivefamilyser vices.com/friendship-most-important-ingredient-in-a-relationship/

Robinson, L., Segal, J., & Jaffe, J. (2021). *Attachment styles and how they affect adult relationships.* HelpGuide.org. https://www.helpguide.org/articles/relationships-communication/attachment-and-adult-relationships htm

Rutherford, T. (2023, July 24). *Financial harmony: Why married couples should work together on their finances.* Life Financial Group. https://www.thelifegroup.org/financial-harmony-why-married-couples-should-work-together-on-their-finances/

Sabrina. (2019, February 6). *15 simple creative ways to show love (plus 30-day relation-ship challenge).* The Budding Optimist. https://buddingoptimist.com/simple-creative-ways-to-show-love/

Sareen Nowakowski, A. (2017, August 24). *5 reasons you should stay with someone you love, even when it seems impossible.* Elite Daily. https://www.elitedaily.com/dating/reasons-to-stay-with-someone-you-love/2053084

Schumer, L. (2021, December 10). *100 fun date ideas to really up the romance.* Good Housekeeping. https://www.goodhousekeeping.com/life/relationships/a31405192/cute-romantic-date-ideas/

Scott, S. J. (2017, December 30). *101 new skills: Learn something new in 2024.* Develop Good Habits. https://www.developgoodhabits.com/new-skills-to-learn/

Segal, J., Smith, M., Robinson, L., & Boose, G. (2023, March 1). *Nonverbal commu-nication and body language.* HelpGuide.org. https://www.helpguide.org/articles/relationships-communication/nonverbal-communication.htm

Seidman, G. (2017). *10 tips for solving relationship conflicts.* Psychology Today. https://www.psychologytoday.com/us/blog/close-encounters/201704/10-tips-solving-relationship-conflicts

Setting financial goals as a couple. (n.d.). More than Money. https://www.nab.com.au/personal/life-moments/family/get-married/budgeting-couple

Sharp, E. M. (2005, September 27). *Openness important for couples of all ages.* Tampa Bay Times. https://www.tampabay.com/archive/2000/04/25/openness-important-for-couples-of-all-ages/

Smith, S. (2015, May 19). *How to stay committed in a relationship: Benefits & tips.* Marriage.com. https://www.marriage.com/advice/relationship/tips-to-maintain-commitment-in-your-relationship/

Stadler, S. (2021, August 11). *Lack of commitment in a marriage.* Unhappy Marriage. https://www.unhappymarriage.info/lack-of-commitment-in-a-marriage/

Starting a family? Take these 10 steps to prepare financially. (n.d.). Fulton Bank. https://www.fultonbank.com/Education-Center/Family-and-Finance/Financially-Prepare-to-Start-a-Family

Stockhausen, R., & Milton, J. (2021, April 7). *14 proven ways to build emotional intimacy in 2023.* Practical Intimacy. https://practicalintimacy.com/how-to-build-emotional-intimacy-relationship/

Strauss, N. (2022, November 20). *Neil Strauss quote.* Quotes. https://www.quotes.net/quote/92404

10 ways to nurture love and friendship in your marriage. (2023, June 7). Rich in Relationship. https://richinrelationship.com/10-ways-to-nurture-love-and-friendship-in-your-marriage/

Tete, S. (2021, August 5). *Conflict in relationships: Causes & best ways to deal with it.* StyleCraze. https://www.stylecraze.com/articles/conflict-in-relationships/

Things that can break trust. (2023, April 25). MorningCoach. https://www.morningcoach.com/blog/things-that-can-break-trust

Tips for couples setting retirement goals. (n.d.). Regions. https://www.regions.com/insights/wealth/retirement/establishing-a-plan/retirement-goals-same-page

Tips for the best way to save money as a couple. (2023, December 24). The People's Federal Credit Union. https://tpfcu.com/blog/tips-saving-money-together-couple/

Urban, T. (n.d.). *Tim Urban quote.* QuoteCatalog. https://quotecatalog.com/quote/tim-urban-and-when-you-ch-badMG01

Varsos, R. (n.d.). *A quote by Reshall Varsos.* GoodReads. https://www.goodreads.com/quotes/7657129-intimacy-is-not-purely-physical-it-s-the-act-of-connecting

Vow renewal checklist: How to plan the perfect day. (2022, July 4). Stationers. https://www.greenvelope.com/blog/vow-renewal-checklist

Warren, S. R. (2020, June 12). *Are you sure you're actually friends with your spouse?* XoNecole. https://www.xonecole.com/being-friends-with-your-spouse/you-can-tell-your-partner-anything

What makes a good relationship? Gratitude, say experts. (2022, February 1). Health

Concepts, Ltd. https://healthconceptsltd.com/2022/02/01/what-makes-a-good-relationship-gratitude-say-experts/

Why understanding love is important for your relationships. (2024, February 21). Better-Help. https://www.betterhelp.com/advice/love/why-understanding-love-is-important-for-your-relationships/

Whyte, W. H. (n.d.). *William H. Whyte quote*. Quotepark.com. https://quotepark.com/quotes/1493226-george-bernard-shaw-the-single-biggest-problem-in-communication-is-the/

Printed in Great Britain
by Amazon

47755647R00076